The Escape Motif in the American Novel
Mark Twain to Richard Wright

*"In a passionate escape
there must be not only a place from which
to flee but a place to which to flee."*

—Sinclair Lewis, *Main Street*

THE ESCAPE MOTIF
IN THE AMERICAN NOVEL ;

MARK TWAIN
TO RICHARD WRIGHT

by Sam Bluefarb

Ohio State University Press

Copyright © 1972 by the Ohio State University Press
All Rights Reserved

Library of Congress Catalog Card Number 73-188738
International Standard Book Number 0-8142-0168-7
Manufactured in the United States of America

TO EVE

CONTENTS

Although it is true that the motif of flight, or escape, appears frequently in American literature, to the best of my knowledge the subject thus far has not been treated in a full-length study. This is what I have set out to do in the following pages.

Further, I decided to limit myself to a discussion of eight novels, beginning with Twain's *Huckleberry Finn* and ending on the threshold of mid-twentieth century with Richard Wright's *Native Son*—the first, a book that, in spite of its raw violence and its portrayal of a corrupt slave society, is filled with hope, extending to the last, in which all hope has fled. I believe that both of these novels, and those in between, go to form a paradigmatic parabola of the escape motif, adequate enough to have made a case, I hope, for the sustained preoccupation with the theme, not only in the novels of our national literature in the late nineteenth century and the first several decades of the twentieth, but in such critical works that have dealt with that motif in our literature.

The scope of this study, then, is selective rather than comprehensive. The works discussed are among some of the more significant and typical examples of the theme of flight, or escape, in the modern American novel. Many more works might have been included to reveal this motif, but the result would have been repetitious rather than revealing, massive rather than searching, broad rather than deep, in the nature of a survey rather than a probe. To compensate partially for any works neglected, omitted, or unconsciously slighted, I have included a two-part Appendix, divided into American novels of the pre-Twain (or pre-*Huckleberry Finn*) period and the novels of the post-Twain period, all of which in one way or another— some only slightly—touch upon an escape of some sort. The second part of the list is, for obvious reasons, the more comprehensive, since it covers the modern post-Twain novel of escape. But this Appendix cannot be looked upon as anything exhaustive (far from it!); and the reader most likely can add many more items to it.

Sam Bluefarb

Wilmington, California

ACKNOWLEDGMENTS

I should like to express my gratitude and appreciation to all those persons whose suggestions and encouragement made this book possible. First to Hamlin Hill of the University of Chicago, I should like to express my thanks for his aid and comfort in the early days of this study. I should also like to extend that word of appreciation to the following: Morris Freedman of the University of Maryland, Weldon A. Kefauver and his associates connected with the Ohio State University Press—especially for their editorial suggestions and encouragement—and all of those nameless (and treasured) human beings too numerous to mention here, who whether they knew it or not, made a difficult path a little less difficult.

For permission to quote from other works, I am indebted to the following: The University of California Press (*Mark Twain and Huck Finn,* by Walter Blair); Harper and Brothers

(*Native Son,* by Richard Wright) ; Viking Press (*Winesburg, Ohio,* by Sherwood Anderson) ; Charles Scribner's Sons (*A Farewell to Arms* and *Green Hills of Africa,* by Ernest Hemingway) ; Viking Press and McIntosh and Otis (*The Grapes of Wrath,* by John Steinbeck) ; *Commonweal* ("A World of Outcasts," by Catharine Hughes) ; Houghton Mifflin Co. (*The Heart is a Lonely Hunter,* by Carson McCullers) ; Chandler Publishing Company (*Adventures of Huckleberry Finn,* by Mark Twain; Facsimile Edition, ed. Hamlin Hill) and Harper and Row, Publishers, Inc.; H. Marston Smith and Elizabeth Dos Passos (*Three Soldiers,* by John Dos Passos) ; Macmillan Co. (*The Dungeon of the Heart: Human Isolation and the American Novel,* by Edwin T. Bowden) ; Yale University Press (*The Innocent Eye: Childhood in Mark Twain's Imagination,* by Albert E. Stone, Jr.) ; Criterion Books (*Love and Death in the American Novel,* by Leslie A. Fiedler) ; Charles Scribner's Sons (*Ernest Hemingway: Critiques of Four Major Novels,* ed. Carlos Baker) ; Rutgers University Press (*The Wide World of John Steinbeck,* by Peter Lisca) ; Stein and Day (*Waiting for the End,* by Leslie A. Fiedler) ; *Daedalus* ("On Emerson," by Robert Frost) ; Oxford University Press (*The Novel and the World's Dilemma,* by Edwin Berry Burgum) ; University of Minnesota Press (*Richard Wright,* by Robert Bone) ; Random House, Inc., Vintage Books (*The Rebel,* by Albert Camus) ; Dennis Dobson (*No Voice is Wholly Lost,* by Harry Slochower).

The Escape Motif in the American Novel
Mark Twain to Richard Wright

chapter one

Introduction:
Some Backgrounds and
Implications of the Escape Motif

The presence of escape, or flight, in the modern American novel has long reflected a dominant mood in American life. Indeed, wherever it appears in American literature—and it does so with astonishing frequency—it appears as a kind of obsessive accompaniment, a counterpoint to, or even a part of, the main structure of the story. The element of escape thrusts back to early American beginnings and beyond to the European past and the flight from Europe itself; mass escape in America (as distinct from individual escape, stressed in the following pages), which historians refer to as migration, reached its high tide in the opening and settling of the frontier and the conquering of the wilderness, or of what Henry Nash Smith has called the Virgin Land—the American West. This move into the West was perhaps the high point of escape from the older civilization, from an older, perhaps even an effete, way of life. But the deep—one might say chronic—urge of Americans to escape did not end with the closing of the frontier or the atrophy of the great optimistic strain in American life that reached its apogee just a few years before the beginning of the Civil War. For while frontiers disappeared and hopes died, the urge to escape—which created both the hopes and the frontiers— continued to exist as if the frontier were still there and as if all hope had not been abandoned. That impulse, because of its tenacity in American life and character, continued in spite of the loss of hope, in spite of the cessation of migration and the closing of the frontier by about 1880.[1] Indeed, the very urge to escape—after the Civil War especially, but most especially in the twentieth century—was born out of desperation and hopelessness, so that escape finally became not so much an act of hope, optimism, and Emersonian self-reliance as of hopelessness and confusion.

Although the novels discussed in the following pages follow a chronological order, there has been no rigid attempt to trace the evolution of escape in the modern American novel strictly in those terms. The chronological design as it appears here is one of convenience rather than of intention; convenience, at least, was the larger consideration. If there seems to be some sort of developmental pattern in the choice, variation, and characterization of escapes and escapers, this development is probably organic rather than managed, part of the development of American life in the last half century or so, and the way our novelists have recorded that life. If there is a loose evolutionary pattern in the development of the modern American novel of escape, it lies in what I have found rather than in what I have sought. However, to deny that some sort of pattern exists, in the manner in which our novelists from Twain to Wright have dealt with the themes of escape, would be to blind ourselves to the changes that have occurred within American life itself. But there *is* a pattern of sorts. And though we would not wish to slight the common roots of all flight in the modern American novel, we must recognize that although flight is the common denominator of these works, the peculiarities of the historical periods that shaped and thrust them forth both into the national consciousness and the national literature also shaped and molded the characteristics of the individual work. Because of this it should be evident that the nature of Huck Finn's escape in the mid-nineteenth century (as the first of significant escapes in the modern American novel of escape) is quite different from, and sharply contrasts with, Bigger Thomas's escape in *Native Son* in the fourth decade of the twentieth century. Although for the most part the need of the escaper is to flee a difficult or dangerous situation, the first escape—Huck's —is still permeated with the optimistic glow so closely associated with the westward advance in America—at least, the time of Huck's escape was filled with optimism; the second is more a blind flight, where what was once an escape into the

West does not push much further than the bounds of Bigger Thomas's labyrinthine ghetto.

Though escape generally implies a flight from one reality to another, escapism has a wider cluster of associations. For escapism implies a flight from daily "reality," [2] far less forgivable than literally running away from a society or situation. Escapism may take as many forms as there are escapists—from drugs and sex to an escape to a South Seas island, as Theron Ware at one point in Harold Frederic's novel longs to do. Usually, in our time, escapism has been exemplified by the passive mass audience and by various groups as represented by the Beats of the nineteen-fifties to the more prevalent and widespread hippies of the sixties and seventies. Where the Beats escaped into a world of disaffiliation, poetry, and pot, the hippies have made escapism itself more than simply a marginal way of life; it has become a life style itself that, in its less injurious forms—dress, hair styles, commercial appeal (psychedelic clothing stores and bookstores)—has been absorbed into the very establishment hippie-ism had set itself up to oppose.

One exception to all of this is made up of the protests and demands of the more vocal—and often violent—expressions of campus radical activists, many of whom turned out to be mutations of the Beat and hippie life styles. In terms of the Beats, however, and the later hippies, it is the dynamics of escapism rather than of true escape that are at work.

This study commences with an investigation of Mark Twain's *Adventures of Huckleberry Finn* (1884)—perhaps the first of the modern escape novels—and ends with an examination of escape in two novels: Carson McCullers's *The Heart Is a Lonely Hunter* (1940) and Richard Wright's *Native Son*, also published in that same year. Although the motif of escape in McCullers's work is certainly not as dominant as it is in

Huckleberry Finn (unless the search for love itself is a form of escape), Jake Blount, the escaper in *The Heart Is a Lonely Hunter,* though not the central character, is still in the main tradition of the escaper in the modern American novel of escape; significantly, however, Jake is an escaper who now no longer has a place to flee to—except down the road, to the next village, the next town, or the next county. The move to the West (as foreshadowed by Huck's flight across to the Territory) has atrophied into the twitch and reflex of the disjointed limb, a move limited to, or contained within, the region in which the original trauma occurred. Thus, there are no longer frontiers that a Jake Blount (or a Bigger Thomas in his black ghetto labyrinth) might explore or strike out for; there is no territory ahead either for a Jake Blount or a Bigger Thomas in the modern American novel of escape. They both now represent escape as a dead end. In a sense, this predicament sums up the major dilemma of our time (in terms of escape, that is), to the extent that the late President Kennedy ingeniously resorted to the campaign slogan of "The New Frontier" in order to dramatize the notion that if the *old* frontier was no longer there, there were at least other frontiers that one might strike out for. But one can be fairly certain that the appeal of the New Frontier, legitimate in its context as it was, had little to do with the business of escape in the following pages. Thus, for Jake Blount—as certainly *not* for Huck Finn —flight is the result of an individual spiritual and social bankruptcy. By the time we get to Jake Blount, the whole pattern of flight in the American novel since *Huckleberry Finn* has come full circle; it has reached dead end. Like Huck, Jake too might well say, "I been there before." Except that in Jake's case, there is no territory that he can light out for ahead of the rest. The territory ahead, as Wright Morris has put it, now lies behind us, in the past. There are no more territories, or, if there are, they have been staked out. And, besides, the Great Depression effectively put an end to the buoyancy, hope, and optimism of the earlier frontier.

And Bigger Thomas in Wright's *Native Son* does not even have the hope that a Jake Blount can nurse, illusory as Blount's hope is. For in contrast to the other escapers discussed in the following pages, Bigger does not even have the solace of hope. He is trapped by his society as the rat he kills in the early pages of the novel is trapped by Bigger.

The opening up of the frontier gave the phenomenon of escape in the modern American novel its peculiarly American stamp. Although the theme of flight may be seen in other literatures, it is only in American literature, particularly in the American novel, that the preoccupation with flight begins to loom large, begins to represent what is most characteristically American—the urge to be forever wandering forward into new territories, to take to the Open Road, as Whitman chronicled that urge, to be on the move, as fictional Americans from Natty Bumppo to Kerouac's Dean Moriarty have enacted it. This American preoccupation—the desertion of the old for the hope of the new—has been a deep and powerful force in American life since the landing of the Pilgrims at Plymouth Rock, in their own escape from social and religious persecution. The stream is not only deep but broad, sweeping along on its current not only escapers from Old World persecution but those escapers-in-reverse of some three centuries later, the expatriates of the 1920s, who look east rather than west in their attempt to escape what was a once-fresh optimism that had since degenerated into plain hucksterism.

In examining flight, or escape, as an American phenomenon, one also sees that Americans were as diverse in the manners in which they chose to flee as the broad diversity of the population from which most of the escapers came. Americans, in their search for the holy (or unholy) grail of raw experience, in their quest for the self through escape, chose a variety of means; for every escape, even in terms of mass migration, was ultimately dependent upon the individual. Ultimately, all escapes are individual, even though the individual at times may himself be part of a larger escape—as were Lieutenant Henry in the retreat at Caporetto and Tom Joad in the westward migration of the Joads and other migrants from the dust bowl. But wherever the escape led, it led further, deeper into life, so that, as such, it rested on no airy philosophizings or aimless wanderings, but on a resolute decision to head *somewhere;* it meant leaving behind the old, or former places, where one not only fled the places but the identities that had grown up and become a part of those places. The move away from the earlier places was entirely pragmatic, bound up with the deep-grained American tradition of going out after something, looking it over— whether a homestead or a wilderness in which to build a home —and trying it out: Thoreau went to the woods; Whitman took to the open road; and Melville went to sea.

One major setting, or perhaps a goal, of escape in America has long been the woods, or the great forests. They are not simply a setting for escape but a haunting symbol of the restless American spirit searching for a quest. From the earliest days of our history as recorded in our literature—whether in the journals of the Pilgrims, the diaries of the Puritans, the notebooks of the gentlemen surveyors out of Virginia, or the more polished, self-conscious literature of Cooper, Irving, and Hawthorne—the woods have stood for something obsessive, mysterious, and, in troubled times, a place to escape into. One either actually went to the woods, as Thoreau did, or vicariously went to them by taking up a novel by Fenimore Cooper or Brockden Brown. From Brockden Brown through Fenimore Cooper and Hawthorne, the forest has sometimes represented the fact and, almost always, the symbol of escape. As I have suggested, the woods not only offered an escape from one form of life, but their image appears and reappears in the writings of Thoreau: one went to the woods in order to plunge further *into* life; for only in the woods could one "front . . . the essential facts of life." To Thoreau the woods beyond Concord represented that temporary escape from Concord—limited as it was —where he could begin to learn something about himself.

As the woods have represented a place to escape to, or even hide in, so each writer brought his own vision to them, a vision that largely determined the manner in which he viewed life. To the literary imagination the woods became a symbol of escape. In much of Hawthorne's work, especially the tales, the woods take on special significance, representing for Hawthorne's characters and symbolizing for us those forbidden freedoms that the pious settlements and their leaders frowned upon: in the tales the woods became the scene of witches' revels, sacrilegious rituals, Maypole merriments, or wilder orgies—in short, the idea made concrete of the revolt against the settlement civilization and the grim deity that presided over that civilization.

In the works of Cooper and Twain, though the woods are still there, they have been pushed farther west and do not seem to frown down upon the trailblazer so threateningly; nor do they reecho any longer with the revels of witches. (Hawthorne, of course, coming after Cooper, dealt with the woods of pre-Cooper times; when Hester Prynne and Arthur Dimmesdale plan their abortive escape from the village of Boston, they go to the woods to do so.) In Cooper the woods have become more attractive, for the reader if not for those who strike out into them. Cooper's hero, whether as Leatherstocking, Deerslayer, or Natty, may be cautious about the woods, for they still pose a threat; but they do so largely in terms of this world rather than the next. The woods are no longer the dark world of the "powers of blackness" run rampant, but a mottled world where nothing more magical is hidden than the cool waters of a rushing spring. There is now room for the play of an occasional shaft of sunlight; and the devil (or devils) that may inhabit that world often turn out to be substantially more material than their predecessors; they may even be a tribe of hostile Indians or a clan of suspicious squatters led by a fierce Ishmael Bush. If the dangers as represented by Indians or squatters are there, they are at least dangers that can be coped with in a manner best suited to *this* world; and if the presence of these forces threatens sufferings, then at least these will be sufferings of a temporary, if not a temporal, nature. Leatherstocking rarely contemplates suffering in its eternal form; it is enough for him if he can take care of those more substantial (if less spiritually consequential) threats to life and limb. Yet Natty considers the woods even less of a threat than the settlements he chronically flees. These to Natty and his various avatars represent the true danger; and one can be fairly sure that, because of this concern in that time of first frontiers, Fenimore Cooper's hero is not merely an early example of the Western hero (to be more weakly melodramatized in the later dime novel), as Henry Nash Smith has suggested,[3] but the prototypal escaper in the modern American novel of escape.

When we get to *Huckleberry Finn,* the woods have taken on a more attractive appeal: they have become idyllic. Huck can now divest himself of all those cramping restrictions of the Widow and Miss Watson, all of those feminizing influences to which even Twain himself was partly victim. The woods now, for the most part, are sunlit, and the Puritan darkness or the less sinister shadows of Indians and squatters have virtually vanished. If there are shadows now, they are likely to be those cast by the shade of a cottonwood offering protection against the heat of the sun to the youngster who has come up from the river or the swimming hole to find cool relief in that shade. In the woods one can pretty much do as he pleases. When Huck is taken by his father into the woods, as much as he fears the man, he is even more happy to leave Saint Petersburg. As he tells us, "It was kind of lazy and jolly, laying off comfortable all day, smoking and fishing, and no books nor study. . . . It was pretty good times up in the woods, take it all around."

But the woods are not the only sanctuary toward which one might direct one's flight, no matter how "lovely, dark, and deep" they may be. At the turn of the century, escape meant a withdrawal *from* the woods, or at least from those clearings in the woods that had become settlements, which in their turn had grown into villages and small towns. Thus, in the late nineteenth and early twentieth centuries escape took the form of what Carl Van Doren had called "the revolt from the village," in which the escaper deserted his own hometown to head for the city, an escape that became dominant both in American life and literature in the first quarter of the twentieth century, and that continues to some degree even to this day. In the following pages, I have attempted to take a closer look at some of these escapes that have become such an intrinsic part of the American legend and certainly of American life itself. If the escape has frequently been self-defeating, that does not invalidate its intensity. On the contrary, the very scope of its failure has often been the measure of its necessity—and even of its pragmatic success in terms of its example to others.

---

1. Frederick Jackson Turner, "The Significance of the Frontier in American History," in *The Turner Thesis Concerning the Role of the Frontier in American History,* ed. George Rogers Taylor (Boston, 1956).

2. As used here, the word is employed in its usual phenomenal sense rather than in all of its fine philosophical shades of meaning.

3. *Virgin Land: The American West as Symbol and Myth* (New York, 1957).

chapter two

Huckleberry Finn:
Escape from Conscience
and the Discovery of the Heart

"All modern American literature
comes from one book by Mark Twain
called *Huckleberry Finn*."

—Ernest Hemingway,
The Green Hills of Africa

The prototypal novel of escape opens on the modern age with Mark Twain's greatest novel, *Adventures of Huckleberry Finn* (1884). Looking back to the place of this novel in the modern American novel of escape, we can see that *Huckleberry Finn* [1]—apart from its stylistic techniques, its realism, its language—is the first modern American novel in which the theme of escape is dominant. All other elements in the work—plot, character, setting, and conflict—are subordinate to this theme. Further, *Huckleberry Finn* has not only a certain "archetypal" value, but seems to be an important starting point for a number of important American novels that follow it. For *Huckleberry Finn* contains all of those ingredients that have gone into the escape novels that have come after it: violence, the difference between the uses of rhetoric and the contrasting realities, conscious and unconscious hypocrisy, gratuitous cruelty—all are included in this novel, but in amounts that may seem immodest or overplayed when we compare the work with the escape novels that follow it. Virtually its entire structure is built upon the escape motif: it touches upon plot, conflict, and symbolic and mythic elements.

Just as *Huckleberry Finn* is the prototypal novel of escape in the modern American novel, so Huck himself is the prototypal escaper. Perhaps Huck's foremost reason for wanting to escape is the high incidence of violence around him—of which he himself is occasionally the target: when Pap Finn, in the throes of the dt's, threatens to kill Huck, the boy escapes by heading for the river. Later, when Huck, in company with the fugitive slave Jim, boards a half-submerged paddle-wheeler, he overhears a conversation between two thieves. The conversation concerns a third member of their group who has threatened to betray the other two. Here the two thieves are trying to decide whether to kill their betrayer or let him stay, trussed up aboard the sinking boat, where, so they hope, nature will take its course. There are the later episodes of the Boggs-Sherburn incident and the Grangerford-Shepherdson feud, which make the previous threats of violence and plans for violence pale by comparison. Next to the otherwise high incidence of violent and painful death, the deaths stemming from the Grangerford-Shepherdson feud are piled up in wholesale quantities.

Initially, Huck is not consciously escaping from all of the hypocrisies, cruelties, and hyper-sentimentalities that accumulate as he moves farther downriver; it is only after he finds himself in the process of escaping from these and more that he consciously begins to grow disillusioned with the shore civilization; only after he sees dogs set afire with turpentine for the amusement of sadistic town loafers, slaves hunted down, men tarred and feathered—only then will Huck feel the need to "light out" from the civilization that countenances such inhuman degradations.

Huck contains within himself all of the urges to flight that will appear in the escapers who come after him. In many ways these too will attempt to escape the same kind of fraud, violence, and hypocrisy that Huck is attempting to flee. We shall see these impulses at work in such escapers as Theron Ware (*The Damnation of Theron Ware*); John Andrews (*Three Soldiers*), and Lieutenant Frederic Henry (of *A Farewell to Arms*). That Huck's first flight is *into* the kind of world his father inhabits—the world of shiftlessness, irresponsibility, and amorality—does not necessarily indicate that Huck is shiftless, irresponsible, or amoral. But when he sees his selfhood threatened—regardless of the sources of the threat—he does not stop to reason, but instinctively takes off for the woods, where a fellow can smoke, fish, swear, and lie around without being bothered by the customs of his (female) civilizers.

There are perhaps as many kinds of escape in *Huckleberry Finn* as there are escapers. These involve not only Huck, but

Jim, and the King and the Duke. These escapes, however, are variations on Huck's. What they do have in common, though, is the desire to shed the restraints and cramping influences of the shore civilization, whether of the slave masters, as in Jim's case, irate townsfolk in the King's and the Duke's, or drab, prosaic realities as in Tom's. But not all of these, of course, are portrayed with equal realism or with equal seriousness, as in the burlesque escape (or Evasion) in the last chapters of the novel; yet within limitations each escape has its purpose. The first of these is Huck's escape from the shore civilization, which takes place in the middle chapters and in the last chapter. These escapes are generally made at night. Huck and Jim, like the fugitives they are, make a practice of "shoving off" after dark. As Huck recounts: "Soon as it was night, out we shoved. . . ." [2] But though Huck's escapes are largely impulsive, determined by the circumstances of the moment—his escape from Pap, his flight to Jackson's Island—Huck occasionally resorts to an ingenuity worthy of the more imaginative Tom Sawyer; indeed, where Tom's notions of escape are derivative and romantic, an enactment of his fantasy life, Huck's are designed to work in the real world. One example of such an "evasion" is his own faked murder.

Jim's escape is of course closely allied with that of Huck. Indeed, it is more dangerous, for if Jim is caught, he may well face hanging as an example to other would-be runaways.

The third of these escapes involves the King and the Duke. Certainly the two frauds, although they have their own unique problems, are forced into escapes that have much in common with those of Huck and Jim: when the King and the Duke find themselves—as they often do—in the act of running away, their escapes are just as urgent for them as are those of Huck and Jim. If they are caught, the consequences, in their own way, will be just as serious.

Besides the variants on Huck's escape embodied in those of the King, the Duke, and Jim, Huck's own escapes alter with the circumstances that precipitate them. Huck's first escape is from the Widow Douglas (the smothering Mom); and though his other escapes may have more of the dramatic element in them, the escape from the Widow, low-keyed as it is, is one of the most significant in the novel; for it is the overcivilizing restraints of the Widow and Miss Watson that Huck must run away from if he is to step into the responsibilities that true freedom and manhood demand.

The escape from Pap is more pressing, more fraught with danger to Huck's physical safety. But if the danger to Huck's freedom as represented by the threat that Pap poses is more immediately pressing than that of the Widow and Miss Watson, what the Widow and her spinster sister represent is potentially more insidious. In the case of these two, the danger is psychological, threatening to Huck's present boyhood and, later, free manhood. In short, in the difference between Huck's half-formed values and the rigid system of beliefs of the two mother figures lies the fulcrum of the novel; that difference represents the essential conflict between Huck and his civilization, the dichotomy between that civilization and the truths that the raft and the river come to represent.

Huck's third escape is from the Grangerford household, with its "aristocratic" code of family pride, its clannishness, its cold cruelty. This escape, however, though perhaps not having the significant implications of the escape from the Widow, is by far the most traumatic of Huck's flights; for he has a genuine liking for the Grangerfords, who seem to be far more decent (to Huck) than either the oversentimental Widow or her starchy sister. They at least possess a certain stoical dignity that neither the Widow nor her sister possesses. Yet, Huck is literally sickened at the bloody skirmish between the Grangerfords and the Shepherdsons:

> It made me so sick I most fell out of the tree. I ain't agoing to tell *all* that happened—it would make me sick again if I was to do that. I wished I hadn't ever come ashore that night, to see such things. I ain't ever going to get shut of them—lots of times I dream about them. (p. 154)

A minor variation on the three previous escapes is that of Huck's escape from the Duke and the King toward the end of the novel. Escape here is not so much brought about by threats to Huck's physical welfare; it is more in the nature of a secession from his participation—or, better, passive compliance—in the fraudulent carryings-on of the rapscallions. In a sense, this is Huck's declaration of independence from the violence, the hypocrisy, and the fraudulence of the shore. When the King and the Duke fall out, Huck feels that it is time for him to light out. As he tells us,

> the minute they was fairly at it, I lit out, and shook the reefs out of my hind legs, and spun down the river road like a deer— for I see our chance; and I made up my mind that it would be a long day before they ever see me and Jim again. (pp. 267–68)

Huck's final escape is of course the oft-cited flight from the "sivilizing" intentions of Aunt Sally. To Huck, Aunt Sally represents—benevolent soul that she is—all of those influences he had escaped from in his initial flight from the Widow Douglas and Miss Watson. In contrast to the prim ways of the Widow and the starchy ways of Miss Watson, each threatening Huck's freedom, the threat that Aunt Sally represents does not grow out of primness or fastidiousness but out of a possessive, oversentimentalized "love." Like Miss Watson and the Widow, Aunt Sally, too, represents a civilization that threatens Huck's freedom as effectively as it restricts that of the black man. Thus, Huck's only alternative is to light out once again for the territory, not only of the land but of the heart.

If the flight from Miss Watson represents Huck's escape from the restrictions of civilization, his attempt to escape from Pap is motivated by far more urgent pressures: escape from the Widow and Miss Watson is precipitated by boredom and the feeling of being closed in; escape from Pap is prompted by Finn's cruelty. Thus, his decision to escape from his father is an immediate consequence of Huck's untenable situation; for the boy is not only a prisoner of Pap (in the literal sense), his very life is imperiled by him. Although it is true that the threats to Huck as represented by Miss Watson and the Widow are threats to his desire for freedom, and, in their way, no less real than those of Pap, Huck nevertheless—realist that he is—has little doubt about which is the more pressing and immediate danger.

Although Huck has thus far only played with the idea of escape, or played *at* escape (as portrayed as early as chapter 1), by chapter 6 he has already begun to consider a genuine and permanent escape—specifically from Pap—as a serious, and perhaps the only, possibility. The alternative of going back to the Widow and being "cramped up and sivilized" is distinctly out of the question now; but remaining with Pap is even less possible. There is no dilemma now; there is only the need for a plan of escape. As he tells us,

> I thought it all over, and I reckoned I would walk off with the gun and some lines, and take to the woods when I run away. I guessed I wouldn't stay in one place, but just tramp right across the country, mostly night times, and hunt and fish to keep alive, and so get so far away that the old man nor the widow couldn't

ever find me any more. I judged I would saw out and leave that night if pap got drunk enough, and I reckoned he would. (p. 48)

Huck is no longer daydreaming—whether of heaven or of hell —but already making carefully calculated plans for escape. Further along in the story, with the growth of their urgency, the plans take on even more calculation and elaboration: "I struck another idea; I judged I'd hide [the canoe] good, and then, stead of taking to the woods when I run off, I'd go down the river about fifty mile and camp in one place for good, and not have such a rough time tramping on foot" (p. 54). At this point Huck begins to conceive of his master plan, not simply for escaping, but for making his escape effective: "I got to thinking that if I could fix up some way to keep pap and the widow from trying to follow me, it would be a certainer thing than trusting to luck to get far enough off before they missed me; you see, all kinds of things might happen" (p. 55). What this master plan finally amounts to involves nothing less than his own "murder." Tom Sawyer's presence—to "throw in the fancy touches"—would make the plan perfect of course.

Although the flight, once decided upon, is, as we have seen, carefully planned, its governing element is more impulsive than reasoned out. Walter Blair suggests that Huck does not rationalize or philosophize about his escape.[3] It is instinctive and impulsive, the threatened organism withdrawing from danger. There is no conscious philosophizing or moralizing behind Huck's flight, and although we are occasionally treated to what appear to be interior monologues—as in Huck's decision to "go to hell"—Huck largely depends on what an older way of life might have referred to as his "better instincts." Thus, the impulse to escape proceeds from two motives: to get away from Pap—who threatens physical destruction—and to get away from the overcivilizing strictures of the Widow Douglas and her sister.

On a less immediate level, Huck's escape from civilization is not merely an escape from the white civilization, or from a slavocracy; it is an escape from the evils which that civilization nurtures, and which transcends the evils of slavery. Further, even if the civilization of the antebellum South would not make "a body sick" at its violence and its false sentimentality, the cant and the fakery it demands for homage would themselves drive a boy like Huck to light out. It is true that Huck's values at the time of his escape are hardly conscious, for he himself is still largely the "slave" of those values of the society. But one need not be a slave in a slave civilization to feel the restraints and the restrictions of that civilization, whatever its nature. The ways of civilization, for Huck at least, cramp the style of a boy who would much rather be out sleeping in the woods where the "old ways [were] best."

Yet, for all his happy barbarianism, Huck is no Rousseauean figure. He may be innately noble, and certainly he has been touched by nature; but he is, after all, the child of the sluggish river civilization from which he attempts to escape. By the time he does escape, he has already been exposed to his society and those of its values that still cling to him. Had Huck never been exposed to the slave society, he might never have come to know the agony (and later, the triumph) involved in the struggles between his society-formed conscience and his heart. It is only when he is finally able to get away from that society that Huck finds happiness, short-lived though it is. And the things that give him happiness make up an idyllic, though prudishly forbidden, catalog: smoking, fishing, floating down-river on a raft, or swimming naked. His plunges into the river, when he runs away from Pap and when he dives off the raft for a swim, become even more pointedly "baptismal." This baptism, or spiritual rebirth, is the first in a line of such immersions; later, other heroes in other countries will take their plunges into rivers to escape their respective predicaments. When we come to John Andrews in Dos Passos's *Three Soldiers* and Frederic Henry in Hemingway's *A Farewell to Arms,* we shall see a kind of ritualistic (connective) link among these escapers.

In its initial stages, Huck's escape is largely impulsive. This, however, does not signify that Huck does not eventually make conscious moral choices in his escapes. Not only do his choices gradually become more moral, but they become more effective in the manner in which they affect him. Within Huck a struggle ensues between society's conscience and his heart, a struggle that begins in those dim, barely conscious areas, but gradually rises to the surface of conscious moral choice as Huck floats farther downriver. Yet, even while all this is taking place, the shore conscience still acts as a powerful censor to Huck's better nature. In considering the step to help Jim in his flight from slavery to freedom, Huck tells himself: "It would get all around, that Huck helped a nigger to get his freedom; and if I was ever to see anybody from that town again, I'd be ready to get down and lick his boots for shame" (pp. 269–70). Huck's decision to write to Miss Watson revealing Jim's whereabouts temporarily puts him at peace with his shore conscience—"I felt good and all washed clean of sin" (p. 271)—until he arrives at his second and more consequential decision.

It is only after Huck's inner morality triumphs over the imposed morality of the shore that his words concerning his letter to Miss Watson come to take on the unstylized honesty of the anti-sermon. There are no long rationalizations now as to what people will think, or why he needs to go and hide his head in shame for "stealing a poor old woman's nigger that hadn't ever done me no harm" (p. 270). Huck remembers Jim's countless acts of kindness and consideration, his concern for his welfare, his loyalty—and he takes the great plunge, not merely from the shore into the river, but from the values of one into the moral imperatives of the other. He does what is, after all, the decent thing, having nothing to do with the "ought" of his society but with the "should" of his own better instincts. If saving Jim from the predators means that he will have to go to hell, then, "all right . . . [he will] *go* to hell."

The relationship between Huck and Jim becomes more mutually dependent the farther from Saint Petersburg they get. As early as chapter 11, Huck's concern for Jim is already one of those impulsive feelings that initially precipitated his own escape. But when Mrs. Loftus tells Huck that Jim is the prime suspect in his, Huck's, "murder," the lad wastes no time in paddling across to Jackson's Island to give Jim the word: "There ain't a minute to lose. They're after us!" (p. 92). On this occasion—the first time Huck shows his concern for Jim— he does not stop to think of him as a runaway slave; rather, he thinks of him as another fugitive, like himself. Indeed, his identification with Jim is so complete that when he tells Jim to "Git up and hump yourself," he does so as one escaper giving urgent instructions to another. For Huck's statement "They're after us!" includes them both. From the moment when Huck tells Jim that the slavehunters are after "us" until he tears up the letter to Miss Watson, Huck's compassion is aroused. It is not merely the compassion of one human being for another less fortunate creature, but of one fugitive for another. Huck, in helping Jim to escape, is expanding the meaning of his own escape. Thus, his escape is meaningful in terms of human freedom itself.

Pap Finn is no small influence on Huck's chronic itch to light out, for Huck is his father's son in more ways than biology alone would account for. Initially, Pap sets the pattern for Huck's later escape values. When Judge and Mrs. Thatcher attempt to reform Finn, he escapes their ministrations, much as Huck later escapes those of Miss Watson, the Widow, and

Aunt Sally. A number of critics, however, have seen Huck's true father (his spiritual father, that is) in the runaway slave, Jim; but some have denied that Jim serves that purpose. However, if there be merit on both sides of the argument, one cannot deny that Pap is not merely Huck's biological father; he is, in his own way, as much Huck's spiritual father as is Jim.

Whereas Huck is attempting to escape a degenerate, if not a venal, society, Pap Finn is attempting to escape that society whose characteristics were already fading away even while they were so much being taken for granted, a settlement society in which the government was beginning to take more of a hand. Pap's tirade against the "gov'ment" for allowing northern Negroes to vote, for denying him jurisdiction over his son, and for keeping him from his "rightful" share of his son's fortune have a familiar ring. The contrasts between a Negro educated in the North and a sottish, illiterate southern white are pointed. Indeed, Finn is a foe of education, as is shown in chapter 5, when he asks Huck to read a passage from a book and follows this by accusing Huck of "putting on frills" when the boy demonstrates his ability to read. Pap wants to escape the "gov'ment" and all those forces that would bend him into a law-abiding citizen. But Finn has degenerated to such an extent that he can only hang around the ragged edges of Saint Petersburg, or thrust into the woods a short distance beyond the town where he can be free from the law and minimum social obligations. His wish to escape a corrupting environment —which has already corrupted him—does not grow into the more vital actions of the westward movement. Pap's spirit is already too moribund for a meaningful escape into the West.

In contrast to Pap's escape, Huck's has wider—and deeper— implications. Here are two aspects of a larger American civilization from which both father and son are attempting to escape. In the father's case, the escape is generally from the meliorative or beneficent aspects of the larger civilization that would eventually free slaves and even at some future date give them the vote! Huck is attempting to escape the same civilization that Pap would flee, but of course for other reasons.

Yet the civilization that can use Jim both as slave and as plaything is "too many" for Huck, whereupon he decides that he has had enough of that civilization. Those last lines of his "book" do not simply refer to a two-week lark with the territory Indians; after all that Huck has been through, his words are much too determined for that. Furthermore, knowing what he is in for, Huck sees those words as having a ring of desperation in them. And so, when Huck tells us that he's "got to light out for the Territory ahead of the rest, because Aunt Sally she's going to adopt me and sivilize me and I can't stand it. [Because] I been there before," we believe him.

1. The shorter title will be used throughout this chapter.

2. Samuel Langhorne Clemens, *Adventures of Huckleberry Finn.* Reprinted by permission of Harper & Row, Publishers, Inc. Page references are to the Facsimile Edition, ed. Hamlin Hill (San Francisco, 1962).

3. *Mark Twain and Huckleberry Finn* (Berkeley, Calif., 1960).

chapter three

Theron Ware:
The Fall from Innocence
and the Escape from Guilt

"What if he did abandon
this mistaken profession of his?"

As the minister of a fundamentalist sect of the Methodist church, Theron Ware, in Harold Frederic's *The Damnation of Theron Ware* (1896), should have been adequately armed with such minimal theology as would have prepared him to recognize the sins of pride, lust, and cupidity; paradoxically, though, his innocence, which leads to his subsequent "damnation," lies in his unawareness of these self-defeating traits. Theron's pilgrimage toward the *terrestrial* city of self-knowledge, therefore, departs from a point in life when he is most ripe for a fall—a fall that will lead to his escape from Octavius and the ministry, and his flight to Seattle. We can thus look upon Theron Ware's escape, nonreligious though it is, as redemptive and partially cleansing in its effect, perhaps his one honest act in the novel.

When Theron first arrives in Octavius, where he has been assigned to a small Methodist church of fundamentalist persuasion, he meets three individuals who are destined to play a decisive role in the drama (and the agony) of his ministry: these are Father Forbes (Theron's Catholic counterpart in Octavius), Celia Madden, one of the priest's parishioners who plays the organ in the Octavius Catholic church, and Dr. Ledsmar, a physician friend of the priest. For Theron these three become a trinity of wisdom, beauty, and knowledge, respectively. In a sense one might call them a kind of "secular trinity," even though it ambiguously includes Father Forbes. Of these three the priest appears to be the most significant figure, for he is a friend of each, and perhaps represents a synthesis of Celia's worship of beauty and Ledsmar's worship of knowledge. Yet Father Forbes goes beyond them, for he has a tolerance for human frailty that the other two do not seem to have. Thus —and there is a symbolic aptness here—Celia Madden (a physically attractive woman) represents beauty; Ledsmar, chilly knowledge—he is something of a Hawthornesque figure; and Father Forbes, pragmatic wisdom.

How do these three—the priest, the girl, and the physician— play such a devastating part in bringing about Theron's fall and his subsequent flight from the town? First, Father Forbes. Though it is true that the priest is, for Harold Frederic's purpose, the voice of Catholicism in Octavius, Forbes' brand of Catholicism is quite liberal, even heterodox. He is not only the preaching priest; he is the urbane scholar discussing religious belief *sub specie aeternitatis:*

> I remember saying to you [Theron] once before, there is really nothing new under the sun. Even the saying isn't new. Though there seem to have been the most tremendous changes in races and civilizations and religions, stretching over many thousands of years, yet nothing is in fact altered very much. Where religions are concerned, the human race are still very like savages in a dangerous wood in the dark, telling one another ghost stories around a campfire. They have always been like that.[1]

But the priest also recognizes the aesthetic values of the church, if only for the reason that they make life more livable for those within the fold who are primarily drawn to the church for its ritual and beauty.

Theron's relationship with Celia Madden is, of course, quite different from that which exists between himself and the priest. In addition to worldly knowledge, Celia represents sexual temptation, which hardly simplifies matters. Indeed, Harold Frederic's sense of artistry and aesthetic symmetry was unimpeachable here: for without Celia Madden to "spice" the story, it might have collapsed under its own dull weight. But Celia is more than an artistic counterpart to Forbes; she plays an essential part in Theron's fall, acting (perhaps consciously) as the Eve-like agent to Theron's Adamic innocence and—later— pride. It is not unexpected, therefore, that the fatal kiss Celia permits Theron—as Theron himself reminds her—was given in the picnic woods outside Octavius. Here, as in Hawthorne a half-century earlier, the woods are a symbol not only of freedom but of those illicitly stolen delights that later leave a stain on the residual conscience. On Theron the effect is to erode what little conscience he has left. Celia's effect on him, then, is probably the most devastating of the three tempters. She has not only made him more aware of the lack of beauty in his life; she has affected him in a much more basic way—through her sexuality. Yet, in the last scene with Celia, toward the end of the book, our feelings are mixed; we both pity and have contempt for Theron. On the one hand, we can understand him without necessarily sympathizing with him: to love well but unwisely is a common human experience; yet we must also see Theron for the proud oaf he is, one who deserves all he gets. Celia affects him not only aesthetically but erotically, and the two quite understandably have become mixed up in Theron's mind. The aesthetic-erotic elements have become so fused by the heat of Theron's passion to break free from the restraints of his church and its simplistic theology that when Celia offers him some Benedictine, and further calls herself a "Greek"—a worshiper of pagan beauties and Eleusinian mysteries—Theron exclaims:

> I want to be a Greek myself, if you're one. I want to get as close to you—to your ideal, that is, as I can. You open up to me a whole world that I had not even dreamed existed. We swore our friendship long ago, you know: and now, after to-night—you and the music have decided me. I am going to put the things out of *my* life that are not worth while. Only you must help me; you must tell me how to begin. (p. 301)

Actually, Celia's aestheticism is rather tame, even shallow, though it does appear bold in terms of the times and the community in which she espouses and practices it. The effect of this aesthetic "paganism" on Theron Ware is devastating. Like Omphale, Celia has made Theron into the slavish worshiper at the loom of (her) beauty, and she becomes for Theron the aesthetic-sexual counteragent to the dullness of Octavius and its brand of Methodism. Thus, for Theron Ware, Celia represents what countless similar temptresses in American literature have represented: bewitching beauty, and even witchcraft itself, with its orgiastic and diabolic ritual in the night-cloaked woods —in short, the revolt against puritanism.

There seems to be something compulsive about Celia's drive for freedom. But Theron, in his innocence, is blind to this possibility: for him, Celia symbolizes unlimited freedom. Possibly, it is this attitude that finally elicits from her those crushing words that bring Theron's Octavian innocence to an irrevocable end: "It is all in a single word, Mr. Ware . . . I speak for others as well as myself, mind you,—we find that you are a bore" (p. 477). Yet it is in this last talk with Theron that Celia betrays the essential puritan in *herself*. Celia Madden is really no more than a self-projected eidolon of the free, aesthetic life. It is difficult to believe that she would ever allow herself the ultimate gesture of feminism in that time of small-town mores, namely, having an affair and, even more in character, flaunting the fact. Her fin-de-siècle stance is no more than that, and she remains throughout—even when she offers Theron a glass of Benedictine (hardly a temptation!)—quite the proper, and ultimately offended, lady, even a prude.

Just as Dr. Ledsmar will prove to be another kind of tempter when he invites Theron into his laboratory, so Celia proves to be a temptress when she invites Theron into her Aubrey Beardsleyan chambers. For if Ledsmar's science is cold and bloodless, Celia's worship of beauty is a cold thing too. Ironically, she herself is repelled by the cold Dr. Ledsmar, but her own aestheticism is itself nothing more than a bait with which to lure the naïve Theron into an alliance against Ledsmar. "I want you on my side [she tells Theron], against the doctor and his heartless, bloodless science" (p. 149). True, Ledsmar is indeed a cold fish; but then, Celia is hardly a paragon of humanistic warmth and compassion herself. She is to art what Ledsmar is to science—a matter of too much head and too little heart. Thus, Celia's interest in Theron is not entirely disinterested. In this tension between Miss Madden and Dr. Ledsmar, we see an allegorical playing-out of the conflict between the sciences and the humanities—though in vastly oversimplified terms.

If, for Theron Ware, Celia Madden is more dangerous than Ledsmar, then Ledsmar is the more diabolic of the two. The physician is a kind of "mad scientist," inducing in the minister a morbid fascination for all he represents. He reminds one of Nathaniel Hawthorne's Aylmer of "The Birthmark"—also a physician, of sorts—though without the suggestion of sympathy that Aylmer elicits. As Celia Madden's chambers seem to epitomize the arty fin-de-siècle studio, so Ledsmar's rooms seem to represent the laboratory of the unhinged scientist obsessed with "truth," even if the discovery of that "truth" leads to the complete destruction of man's moral foundations. In one part of his house are bookcases, and "the corners of the floor [are] all buried deep under disorderly strata of papers, diagrams, and opened books. One could hardly walk about without treading on them" (p. 322). Elsewhere there are "dark little tanks containing thick water, a row of small glass cases with adders and other lesser reptiles inside, and a general collection of boxes, jars, and similar receptacles connected with the doctor's pursuits. Further on was a smaller chamber, with a big empty furnace, and shelves bearing bottles and apparatus like a drug-store" (pp. 328–29). Ledsmar's house is a depository of the pathologically obsessive—the world's knowledge gone berserk.

Theron Ware's problem does not lie so much in an intellectual attempt to reconcile faith with science, but in the deeper problem of his coming to terms with his own pride. As compared with those who have found some sort of security in an older, more knowledgeable—perhaps more serviceable—faith, Theron is unprepared to handle the hazards of the world. Certainly, his brand of Methodism, unlike that of the hardy Dinah Morris in George Eliot's *Adam Bede,* has hardly given him that ability, or prepared him for the world. Because Theron's intellectual background has been inadequate, he is totally unprepared to handle the problems that the world thrusts upon him as a challenge to his flimsy doctrines and even flimsier beliefs in them. Unlike the Forbeses, the Maddens, and the Ledsmars —whom it is difficult to think of as having their own periods of innocence—Theron's innocence has never received its own immunization against a spiritually diseased world.

After a number of sessions with the priest and the doctor, Theron decides that his meeting them has been a turning point in his life; for he has come to see them as the antithesis of the dominant—and unlettered—minority within his own church. Where the minority represents narrowness and bigotry, Forbes and Ledsmar represent sophistication and skepticism; where the minority would imprison Theron within a deadening, and deadly, conformity, the priest and the doctor would free him for greater knowledge. Thus, "Nothing was clearer to [Theron's] mind than . . . that his meeting with the priest and the doctor was the turning-point in his career. They had lifted him bodily out of the slough of ignorance, of contact with low minds and sordid, narrow things, and put him on solid ground" (p. 197). But whatever might be said of Ledsmar and Celia Madden, it is Father Forbes, with his Bishop Blougram apologetics, who turns Theron's head intellectually—or at least makes such an overwhelming impression on Theron that the minister completely loses his head. The priest, of course, is a greater realist than his friends, Ledsmar and Celia Madden; in truth, it is he who even represents a healthy balance to the intellectual excesses of the doctor and the false—even sentimental—aesthetics of the young woman. In this he comes close, as I have suggested, to Robert Browning's Bishop Blougram, though perhaps with a lesser dose of cynicism in him than Browning's shrewd, worldly bishop.

The split between soul and mind in Theron soon becomes apparent: "He had passed definitely beyond pretending to himself that there was anything spiritually in common between him and the Methodist Church of Octavius" (p. 199). The step from contempt for others to the elevation of oneself is a short one: not long after, Theron decides that there is really no spiritual bond between himself and the "low minds" of his congregation, for he has begun to see himself as a kind of genius. If—according to Theron—one of the marks of genius is a predisposition for contracting unfortunate marriages, then Theron finds that he too fits into that category. Hadn't he, in marrying the rather dull, if loyal, Alice, contracted such a marriage? Further, his pride encourages in him an envy of those who have not married. He sees Forbes and Ledsmar as perfect examples of the free, if celibate, life; they can give themselves up to the study of literature and philosophy, and dedicate themselves to the loftiest thoughts without troubling themselves with more mundane things. Not married bliss but single blessedness is what Theron sees as his great loss. All of these forces, when added up, do not make so much for damnation as for a (rather limited) fall. If Theron is damned, then the word ought to be placed within quotation marks, since, at the end of the novel and his stay in Octavius, Theron is better able to handle himself in his confrontation with his own weaknesses and the world that was partly responsible for them than he was at the beginning of the novel.

With the kiss Celia Madden has permitted Theron in the woods outside Octavius, Theron's fall is virtually complete; the kiss in the pagan woods bears pagan fruit. For Theron has begun to identify that experience with a growing affinity for pantheistic nature. Theron Ware is no longer a minister in the full sense of that word, *ministering* to the needs of his flock; he has become a worshiper of nature. He will no longer worship God, or even the Deists' God in nature; instead, he will worship the moon, which he has come to identify with Celia Madden. Harold Frederic makes this vivid by having Theron stroll out into the woods on a moonlit night, ostensibly to offer up a prayer of thanksgiving to God for making it possible for him to meet Celia. But the sacred intention is nullified by the profanity of his pagan inclinations:

> The impulse to kneel, there in the pure, tender moonlight, and lift up offerings of praise to God, kept uppermost in his mind. Some formless reservation restrained him from the act itself, but the spirit of it hallowed his mood. He gazed up at the broad luminous face of the [moon]. "You are our God," he murmured. "Hers and mine! You are the most beautiful of heavenly creatures, as she is of the angels on earth. I am speechless with reverence for you both." (p. 390)

During this period of lunar worship, Theron begins to consider the possibilities for his escape from the ministry. Thus, for the first time during his stay in Octavius, he has begun to face the possibility that he may not be fitted for a religious calling. It would be better to resign immediately than to be ousted under an ignominious cloud later, when—as it would appear inevitable—his indiscretion in the woods would be discovered. It is at this point that Theron begins to think of moving out while it is still possible to do so without scandal.

> What if he did abandon this mistaken profession of his? On its mental side the relief would be prodigious, unthinkable. But on the practical side, the bread-and-butter side? For some days Theron paused with a shudder when he reached this question. The thought of the plunge into unknown material responsibilities gave him a sinking heart. He tried to imagine himself lecturing, canvassing for books or insurance policies, writing for newspapers—and remained frightened. But suddenly one day it occurred to him that these qualms and forebodings were sheer folly. Was not Celia rich? Would she not with lightning swiftness draw forth that checkbook, like the flashing sword of a champion from its scabbard, and run to his relief? Why, of course. It was absurd not to have thought of that before. (p. 393)

Where Theron's search for a viable faith had led him from extreme fundamentalism to a superficial and shallow rationalism, now, not having found that faith, he rejects all that the old faith implies. For Theron, one is either "good and straight and sincere," as he had once thought himself to be, or "rotten to the core," as he now thinks of himself. Such has been Theron's simplistic two-valued orientation to his faith. Sister Soulsby, a member of Theron's church, is the complete antithesis of a Father Forbes; she is a simple "soul," relatively unlettered, but possessing a hard practicality; she makes no great claims on her religion. For although she is a person who does not have the learning of a Forbes (one might add, however, that these two share a certain realism), the culture of a Celia Madden, or, at a most unlikely remove, the "science" of a Ledsmar, she ultimately turns out to be Theron's only true friend. Upon Theron's return from his drunken escapade in

New York City after his rejection by Celia, Sister Soulsby attempts to brace up his low spirits:

> "I've told you my religion before. . . . The sheep and the goats are to be separated on Judgment Day, but not a minute sooner. In other words, as long as human life lasts, good, bad, and indifferent are all braided up together in every man's nature, and every woman's too. You weren't altogether good a year ago, any more than you're altogether bad now. You were some of both then; you're some of both now. . . . Nobody is rotten to the core." (pp. 499–500)

In these words there is much more than a touch of the kind of pragmatic wisdom that comes of having been exposed to hardship. Certainly, the Soulsbys—both Mrs. and her husband—having been itinerant sideshow performers, have had a checkered career. Their pragmatism involves a view of life that will not permit any excessive idealization either of life's pitfalls or of its possibilities. Although they do not see life steadily or whole, they are at least aware that learning comes as much from experience as from books. Consequently they can accept the world for what it is rather than for what they would like it to be. And they are never too proud to admit a certain complicity in the world's duplicity. In this they are much more "human" than Theron, for they have the ability to compromise where compromise does no great harm either to themselves or to others.

Until his final escape from Octavius and the ministry, Theron's urges to flee have not been entirely unacted-upon. His early gestures, though tentative, have been made as far back as his boyhood on the farm. Born and reared on the farm, Theron has seen the ministry not merely as a dedication but as an escape from the drab monotony and drudgery of farm life. Thus, even as far back as his transition from farmer to minister, one can already see the seeds of discontent that will later blossom into the full flower of flight. For "neither his early strenuous battle to get away from the farm and achieve such education as should serve to open to him the gates of professional life, nor the later wave of religious enthusiasm which caught him up as he stood on the border-land of manhood, and swept him off into a veritable new world of views and aspirations, had been a likely school of merriment" (p. 29). Even before his marriage to her, Theron sees in Alice a possible avenue of escape:

> She was fresh from the refinements of a town seminary: *she read books; it was known that she could play upon the piano.*[2] Her clothes, her manners, her way of speaking, the readiness of her thoughts and sprightly tongue,—not least, perhaps, the imposing current understanding as to her father's wealth,— placed her on a glorified pinnacle far away from the girls of the neighborhood. (p. 27)

If, from the first moment of his arrival in Octavius, Theron has no *conscious* urge to escape, he has at least begun to give way to a wistful yearning. Discouraged by his first interview with the trustees of the Octavius church, Theron already feels like running away. On this occasion the trustees inform him where they stand on such matters as flower-bedecked "bunnits" and their antagonism toward "book-learnin' or dictionary words in [the] pulpit" (p. 43). They go on to tell him that "no new-fangled notions can go down here. Your wife'd better take them flowers out of her bunnit afore next Sunday. . . . What we want here, sir, is straight-out, flat-footed hell,—the burnin' lake o' fire an' brimstone. Pour it into 'em, hot an' strong" (pp. 43–44).

Theron's escapes, or what have thus far been proclivities, are as yet not consciously conceived in explicit physical terms or plans. He would like to "learn a trade," write a book, enjoy a

certain solitude (as he actually succeeds in doing when he contracts some vaguely defined, probably psychosomatic, illness).
But he does not even begin to contemplate an actual escape in
terms of geographical flight until the end of the book, an escape that also coincides with the end of his year in Octavius.

For some months before his urge to escape becomes a conscious plan, Theron, still the minister, desires to make the best
of both worlds: to enjoy his position as minister—with all of
the respect and regard such a position exacts from others—and
to indulge his whims. But this conflict of interests sets him up
as an excellent target for his own self-destructive urges. This
kind of fence-straddling is then untenable. Sooner or later he
must decide which it is to be—the "buried life" in Octavius or
escape from it; sooner or later he must translate his urges into
action.

His first plan is of course the dead-end plan of an escape
with Celia. Yet, blind as it is, both as to its possibilities and
consequences, it *is* one of the first signs that Theron is now
consciously planning an escape of some sort; the circumstances
of his wife and the church, both to whom and to which he is
"married," lead him consciously into the practical considerations of such a projected flight:

> But he could not enter upon this beckoning heaven of a future
> until he had freed himself. When Celia said to him "Come!" he
> must not be in the position to reply, "I should like to, but un-
> fortunately I am tied by the leg." He should have to leave Oc-
> tavius, leave the ministry, leave everything. He could not begin
> too soon to face these contingencies. (pp. 394–95)

In this early, consciously considered escape, then, we see what
later turns out to be the great impulse that not only will take
Theron Ware out of Octavius, but out of a way of life he had
heretofore (until his arrival in the town) resigned himself to.

These early considerations of escape have taken three forms: first, his desire to escape from the church and its ministry; second, his desire to escape from Alice and what he feels to be an unfortunate marriage; and third, his desire to escape his former (innocent) self. Theron pleasurably indulges in one of these fantasies on the train that is taking him to New York City and to what he hopes will be a critical and successful reunion with Celia Madden. Peering out the window, he sees a rich man's yacht that will take them both to those happy isles of blissful irresponsibility:

> Ah, how the tender visions crowded now upon him! Eternal summer basked round this enchanted yacht of his fancy,—summer sought now in Scottish firths or Norwegian fiords, now in quaint old Southern harbors, ablaze with the hues of strange costumes and half-tropical flowers and fruits, now in far-away Oriental bays and lagoons, or among the coral reefs and palm-trees of the luxurious Pacific. He dwelt upon these new imaginings with the fervent longing of an inland-born boy. Every vague yearning he had ever felt toward salt-water stirred again in his blood at the thought of the sea—with Celia. (p. 454)

If the yacht represents for Theron an escape from responsibility, it also suggests the Edenic idyll of innocence that has been the staple of American fiction since Melville's *Typee*. Of course, Theron's dream of escape with Celia on such a yacht (symbol of the ideal escape?) is in the realm of pure fantasy, because it is based on nothing more substantial than Theron's innocent vision of the world. Yet—and we might call this a fault of hyper-imagination in Theron—fantasy that it is, it nevertheless represents for this minister *manqué* a sharp and pleasant contrast to the drab-hued existence of his life in Octavius.

Throughout the year in Octavius—a year that for Theron represents a spiritual lifetime—the minister, whether he has known it or not, has been attempting to flee the mask toward his truer (perhaps better) self. Because Theron Ware had thought of himself as possessing a kind of Edenic goodness, when he finally discovers a side of himself that he had never thought existed, the knowledge almost kills him. As Sister Soulsby puts it, "Whatever else he does, he will never want to come within gunshot of a pulpit again. It came too near murdering him for that" (p. 506).

Theron Ware, having finally learned a lesson, can now turn his back on the past and look toward the future and a new way of life. Disabused of his outworn illusions, he can now face a new life in a new country. For Theron, the year has come full circle, and, looking toward the future, he can now decide to take his chance in the West—Seattle—where he will build a new life, perhaps even go into politics. To Alice, Seattle *"sounds* like the other end of the world," which of course, in a sense, it is. And even more than that, Seattle represents for Theron not only the "other end of the world" but a new world. Like all of those escapers extending back into the American past, Theron is also in the tradition of the escaper who, if he is to survive as an individual and a human being, *must* strike out into the "wilderness" of a new life. For Theron, as for Huck and Deerslayer before him, the restrictive settlements have closed in, and he must "light out," if he is to save himself from an even greater calamity than he has already experienced.

The final scene—that of Theron's departure for the West— takes place in the spring, signifying renewal and the rebirth of hope. Like George Willard, who also takes his leave of the old life in the spring, Theron will depart (or escape) in a season of promise. Thus, *The Damnation of Theron Ware,* though a story of a fall, is really the story of a fortunate fall (even if "fortunate" in a highly qualified sense). For Theron has left his greater innocence behind in Octavius; he has grown to

larger manhood, with a more mature knowledge of the world—
namely, a knowledge of his limitations.

1. Harold Frederic, *The Damnation of Theron Ware, or Illumination*
(Chicago, New York, 1896), p. 357. All further quotations are from this edition, published by the Herbert S. Stone Co.

2. Italics added. It is interesting to note that these very words could apply
to Celia Madden later in the story. Having at last begun to identify his wife
with his drab ministry, Theron sees in Celia all of the glamour, the beauty,
and the excitement he had once seen in Alice; for Celia too "reads books,"
and plays a musical instrument—an organ in Father Forbes's church.

chapter four

George Willard:
Death and Resurrection

"I just want to go away. . . ."

Like *Adventures of Huckleberry Finn* and *The Damnation of Theron Ware,* Sherwood Anderson's *Winesburg, Ohio* contains its own pattern of escape. However, in approachnig this work, I have not blinked the fact that, by the strict application of techniques and criteria of the novel, *Winesburg, Ohio* is not a novel at all; it is—at least on the surface—a collection of tales, or episodes, strung together on intertwining threads of contiguous memories that involve a given time and place: a small town in Ohio in the late nineteenth century.

George Willard, in *Winesburg,* may be compared to Nick Adams in Hemingway's *In Our Time* (1925): the two young men grow to maturity by encountering a series of confrontations with life—sometimes "initiatory," [1] sometimes in less traumatic "rituals of passage." But though Nick Adams is the central character of Hemingway's collection of stories, he does not serve as a focal point for the other characters. George Willard, on the other hand, is not only the most sustained character in Anderson's work, but also the reflecting agency by which the other characters in the town see themselves. In making Willard the repository for their problems, the characters in *Winesburg, Ohio* are able to gain some greater—if admittedly still small—insight into those problems. Further, by their confidences George Willard is able not only to gain some insight into the problems of his fellow townsmen but to learn something about himself.

Some of these stories may indeed be capable of standing alone and still make some sense. But fitted together into a larger work, as they are, they have been given a significance and a strength of meaning such as they otherwise could not have had. [2] It is true that some have occasionally been published as autonomous stories. But if there is any doubt that Anderson meant *Winesburg* to be anything less than a single, unified work, then the introductory "Book of the Grotesque" should dispel that doubt; for it is plainly meant to function as the introduction to a longer work, and, indeed, makes more sense in those terms, containing within itself the seed of all that is to flower in the later episodes.

The main character in "The Book of the Grotesque" is a writer; he is not a young man like George Willard, but an old man who has already spent the larger part of his life in the town. He is, in a sense, the George Willard who never left home, but has stayed on to record, bardlike, the buried lives of his people. Although he is not Willard, he seems to act as a kind of anticipatory persona for George. For the old writer has written a book (unpublished) very much like the book George —or, indeed, Anderson himself!—will later write. The book concerns the town and the old man's neighbors. Like the characters in Winesburg, the people in the introductory "Book of the Grotesque" are the stunted fractional men and women of the larger work, *Winesburg, Ohio*. As the "I" in "The Book of the Grotesque" tells us,

> In the beginning when the world was young there were a great many thoughts but no such thing as truth. Man made the truths himself and each truth was a composite of a great many vague thoughts. All about in the world were the truths and they were all beautiful.
>
> The old man had listed hundreds of the truths in his book. I will not try to tell you of all of them. There was the truth of virginity and the truth of passion, the truth of wealth and of poverty, of thrift and profligacy, of carelessness and abandon. Hundreds and hundreds were the truths and they were all beautiful.
>
> And then the people came along. Each as he appeared snatched up one of the truths and some who were quite strong snatched up a dozen of them.
>
> It was the truths that made the people grotesques. The old man had quite an elaborate theory concerning the matter. It was his notion that the moment one of the people took one of the

truths to himself, called it his truth, and tried to live his life by it, he became a grotesque and the truth he embraced became a falsehood.[3]

Although it is true that George Willard is not the main character of the stories, he acts as a unifying agent for the larger work. If there were still some doubt as to the function of George Willard in *Winesburg, Ohio,* that doubt should be quickly dispelled when one comes to the last story, "Departure." It is in this story that George, in leaving Winesburg, will tie up the loose ends of his life there in order "to meet the adventure of life" in the big city (p. 302). Only if we see the town and George's past in it as the "background on which [he is] to paint the dreams of his manhood" (p. 303) can we see this story in its proper relationship to those that precede it: the causes of George's departure are all there in the earlier chapters. That George leaves for parts unknown—the west-bound train he takes suggests he is bound for Chicago—is of no great importance. But his departure certainly is, for he will be able to look back on the town of his boyhood and youth with greater detachment; he will thus be able to see it not only more clearly and objectively but also more sympathetically.

In *Winesburg* George Willard is a representative figure who typifies all of the buried yearnings of his fellow townsmen, but unlike most of them, George finally manages to succeed in escaping the town. His escape, however, signalizes the death of his boyhood and the birth of his manhood. Like the chrysalis of the emerging butterfly, Winesburg has nurtured and prepared the young man for the breakout from the shell of its dead past into the new life of the future.

Willard, however, cannot be seen as a representative type except against the backdrop of the past and the small town that has for so long been symbolic of it. The small town in American literature has been a pervasive presence, ever since that literature broke out of its own colonial chrysalis and became a collection of regional literatures that contributed to the larger national literature. Our writers, for the most part, approached the small town with mixed emotions, depending on their own experience either as young people growing up in small towns or as adults forced to live in, endure, or escape them. The spectrum is broad: from Edgar Watson Howe's embittered memories, as recorded in his *The Story of a Country Town,* to Zona Gale's sentimental *Friendship Village.* No theme in American literature has held the imagination of our writers more firmly than has that of small-town life. Such once-obsessive themes as the fall from innocence, the initiation, and the escape itself have for a long time been subordinate to that of the small town and its impact on the emerging conscience. Anderson's Winesburg is, of course, one of the prime examples of that life.

Peeling off the outer layers of these lives in Winesburg, Anderson, in episode after episode, reveals what are essentially layers of respectability—or the appearance of it—to show us the core of reality that lies at the heart of the town. But if one cannot communicate, or find some degree of surcease from the loneliness in the consummation of a relationship with another, there is always of course, either in the first or last resort, the "out" of escape from those restrictions, an escape that Willard will eventually make. Insofar as he is more sensitive and articulate [4] than the others in the town, George is also different. And it will be this difference that will eventually precipitate his escape from a place and a way of life where, though eccentricity and difference are not difficult to find, they still serve to arouse suspicion. Indeed, it is frequently by his contacts with the alienated souls in the town that George is permitted the partial insights that will lead to his maturity.

Thus, although George Willard may have much in common with his fellow townsmen, sharing in their grotesqueries (though to a lesser degree), he stands apart from them. When we first meet him in the story "Hands," Willard is barely out of adolescence. But if he is barely out of adolescence then, most of the other characters in the book have already reached the fag end of life, chronologically and psychologically, when we first encounter them. George Willard is, of course, more literate than the others, and more articulate, not so much because he can read and write better than they—he is a reporter on the *Winesburg Eagle*—but because he is more sensitive. Where many of his "grotesque" neighbors are self-centered, obsessed by their own personal problems to the point of psychosis, Willard, although he also has his problems, is never so absorbed by them that he cannot look at the world and his neighbors and take stock of both with relatively greater objectivity. He is a sensitive receiver, absorbing all of those impressions with which he will later come to "paint the dreams of his manhood" on the canvas of his small-town youth. George, in being sensitive to the drift of things in the town, not only is articulate in his sensitivity but, through it, shows the makings of a poet. Yet it is not so much the poet or the man of articulation that draws the eccentrics, the freaks, and the "queers" to George; it is finally his sensitivity. To them Willard is a healer.

Further, whereas George is fairly articulate, his fellow townsmen find it difficult to express themselves other than through wild outbursts or inchoate gesticulations. It is only when he is on the verge of making his escape from the town that George can "think through" his own relationship with his neighbors and see them through that mixture of pity and scorn with which a young man of slightly superior talents may look upon those who are educationally inferior to him.

Perhaps more than anyone else in town, George's mother,

Elizabeth, hopes to mold, or remold, her son closer to her heart's desire. Thus, she vicariously wishes to satisfy a yearning that had burned briefly in her young womanhood, and then had flickered out in the "airless" small-town existence that has destroyed the hopes and the lives of many of her neighbors. No longer able to nurture her own dreams—to escape Winesburg to join a company of itinerant actors—Elizabeth Willard has now superimposed something of her own unfulfilled ambitions onto George. She now thinks of him as that remnant of her own youthful self that has not died and that still seeks to find its way out of the buried life into the sunlit world "above the surface."

George's relationship with his father, Tom Willard, is not quite as close as his relationship with his mother. But Tom Willard has also been disappointed by life. He is the proprietor of the New Willard Hotel, which has seen better days and which symbolizes for Tom Willard all of the larger disappointments of his disappointed life. Instead of fulfilling the promise that it had once held for him, it is now a gnawing reminder of the promise that has been broken.

> The hotel was unprofitable and forever on the edge of failure and he wished himself out of it. . . . As he went spruce and businesslike through the streets of Winesburg, he sometimes stopped and turned quickly about as though fearing that the spirit of the hotel . . . would follow him even into the streets. "Damn such a life, damn it!" he sputtered aimlessly. (pp. 24–25)

For Tom Willard the hotel is a symbol not merely of the failure of his life generally but, more specifically, the failure of his domestic life. His recourse is to reach outward to that therapeutic panacea, or escape, of the American male who, defeated in the home, turns outward to those socially acceptable alternates of business or politics. For the most part Tom Willard's escape into local politics is virtually the only escape he is capable of. He still vaguely hopes that he will someday recoup his losses, i.e., his integrity as a man—he is "the leading Democrat in a strongly Republican community" (p. 25)—perhaps getting himself elected to Congress, or even someday becoming Governor. Until then he will vest some of that hope in George.

Tom Willard hopes to justify his own faith in George by contributing the paternal influence toward George's success. But this ambition is not without its snags, for in Tom Willard's attempts to influence George, to capture some of the son's affection if not respect, the rivalry between Tom and his wife for George's love and respect comes to a head. Each wishes for the boy something that neither has had: fulfillment in some sort of success. The form which that success is to take is objectively irrelevant. The locus of irritation lies in the rivalry between the two parents for the possession of the boy's soul. It is a rivalry, of course, that is overwhelmingly reminiscent of another father-mother rivalry in the modern novel, that of Gertrude and Walter Morel in D. H. Lawrence's *Sons and Lovers*. The parallel between the two situations—both patently Oedipal—suggests, as some critics have noted, Anderson's debt to Lawrence in his use of the earlier writer's theme.

George's ambition to become a writer—as distinct from being a newspaper reporter—is obviously the manifestation of a far greater drive within him than even Elizabeth can control. Apart from literary ambitions, George feels the compulsion to make something of himself. As the boy develops into manhood, he finds that he must free himself for greater things than common expectations; and he must do so in his own way. Paradoxically, each of the parents wants for George what George wishes for himself. But he cannot be pressured into his encounter with the world; he must do it in his own way, at his own pace. It is significant that George's decision to leave Winesburg, to pursue his own course with a minimum of parental interference, is made early in the book, long before the death of his mother. Early in the book, perhaps to prepare her for the inevitable, George tells Elizabeth of his intentions:

> Sitting in a chair beside his mother he began to talk. "I'm going to get out of here," he said. "I don't know where I shall go or what I shall do but I am going away."
>
> The woman in the chair waited and trembled. An impulse came to her. "I suppose you had better wake up," she said. "You think that? You will go to the city and make money, eh? It will be better for you, you think, to be a business man, to be brisk and smart and alive?" She waited and trembled.
>
> The son shook his head. "I suppose I can't make you understand, but oh, I wish I could," he said earnestly. "I can't even talk to father about it. I don't try. There isn't any use. I don't know what I shall do. I just want to go away and look at people and think."
>
> .   .   .   .
>
> She wanted to cry out with joy because of the words that had come from the lips of her son, but the expression of joy had become impossible to her. "I think you had better go out among the boys. You are too much indoors," she said. "I thought I would go for a little walk," replied the son. . . . (pp. 36–37)

The dialogue sets the tone for the relationship between George and his mother and shows the kind of restlessness that George has inherited from her. As one can see from this exchange, Elizabeth's feelings are, to say the least, mixed. But her love for her son gives more than it takes (a giving symbolized by the $800 with which she unsuccessfully attempts to finance George's exodus from Winesburg); for in George's stated purpose, to "go away," Elizabeth seems to see some sort of vicarious resolution for her own girlhood restlessness;

in George's escape, she too—like her husband—will enjoy a "reprieve" from the stagnation of their lives.

In spite of Elizabeth's concern for George's freedom of action, her concern for George is one expression of concern for herself, for the satisfaction of her own desires. Like those other townspeople who burden George with their problem and presences, there is something vampiric about Elizabeth's relationship with her son. Like any form of possessiveness, it must finally demand for its love object what it wishes for itself. Only in Elizabeth's death will George find complete release from whatever domination she has held over him. Like Elizabeth, Tom Willard the father is parasitical too, for like her, he also wishes for George what he had wished for himself —fame and glory. Both parents wish nothing more than to create, or re-create, in George the realization of their own image of what he ought to be.

As long as he remains in Winesburg, George Willard is the recipient of the confidence of the townspeople. Through these confidences he is slowly impressed with the private agonies that go on inside the hearts of even the most hardened types in the town. George, however, in playing the part of a Miss Lonely-hearts, will only go on playing that part to the extent that he is able to stand up under the constant assaults on his increasingly raw and hyperactive sensibilities. But he cannot go on like this indefinitely; when he reaches the point where he can no longer stand the town and the stunted souls who inhabit it, he will leave. Unlike Nathanael West's Miss Lonelyhearts, also a news reporter, George will not be—indeed, is incapable of making himself—the Christ figure for the burdens of others. For in fleeing the town George will save *himself* from the kind of Christlike immolation—another aspect of the "grotesque"— that West's character eventually submits to. In wishing to flee the "buried lives" of his fellow townsmen, George also wishes to flee those lives because they are constant irritants, constant reminders of his own buried life. He will occasionally bear the unburdening of these sick souls, and will even help them to alleviate their burdens. (Perhaps this is one way he can keep from becoming a "grotesque" himself.) But he can only continue to do so at the risk of dissipating his own energies, energies he will need for his own breakout from Winesburg and the struggle with the world beyond it.

There is at least one way in which George Willard expands his knowledge of the world—apart from his experience—and that is through books. This bookish knowledge may be seen as something that will permit him to impose some sort of pattern on his life and even, perhaps, on the lives of those around him. Some of these books tell of the Middle Ages—a flight back into the past. But this is only the reverse of his later escape, into the future. His interest in the Middle Ages at this stage suggests that the nature of George's escape is an inverted one—for the moment. Significantly enough, his interest in the Middle Ages suggests another facet of George's evolving personality—his romanticism. Yet the mooning romantic reading and dreaming about the Middle Ages must sooner or later break out into the world that he inhabits, the world that offers living experience. It must draw George out of the world of boyhood that he still, dreamlike, lives in, to thrust him into manhood.

In "An Awakening" we view a partial initiation of George from boyhood into manhood. In this episode one of these minor, or partial, initiations will start the machinery of George's escape mechanism moving and will prove to be the beginning of his explicit attempt to escape the town. This initiation comes about through the humiliation young Willard suffers at the hands of Ed Handby, the local bartender. It is this experience that brings George to one of the critical junctures of his "awakening"—the beginnings of true manhood—to the knowledge of his own limitations. In George's attempt to experience an adult sexual relationship with Belle Carpenter, a woman of the town, he is paradoxically made aware that he is still very much a boy. For Ed Handby, who unceremoniously breaks in upon that attempt, does not even deign to fight with George to assert his rights over Belle (who is only using the innocent young Willard as a pawn in her battle to bring back the jealous Handby to her). Handby not only will not dignify young Willard by challenging him to a fight, he thrusts George aside like a whipped puppy:

> The bartender did not want to beat the boy, who he thought had tried to take his woman away. He knew that beating was unnecessary, that he had the power within himself to accomplish his purpose without using his fists. Gripping George by the shoulder and pulling him to his feet, he held him with one hand while he looked at Belle Carpenter seated on the grass. Then with a quick wide movement of his arm he sent the younger man sprawling. . . . (pp. 225–26)

Ed Handby picks Belle Carpenter up off the grass and "marches" her away, having proven his own manhood in the face of young Willard's impotence. Thus, this incident, perhaps more than any other, paradoxically brings George to the beginnings of manhood—by convincing him that he is still a boy with a boy's limitations. He finds neither physical nor romantic love in the Winesburg of his youth, for he is too puny to battle a full-grown man, and he is too timid to make love to a mature woman. As for Helen White, his sweetheart, she is still the object of Willard's boyish crush that may later develop into something more substantial but at this time is still in its idyllically romantic stage.

When George arrives back in town after the humiliating incident, he runs along a street of frame houses and begins to realize something he had never quite sensed before: for the first time he sees how squalid, miserable, and hopeless these streets and houses are. In this moment, through these "objective correlatives" of frame houses, the meanness and the futility of the town are crystalized for George. The houses now seem to bring out all of the meanings that heretofore had lain hidden from him. Not only do they crystalize the meaning of the town for George, but they appear as symbols of all the closed doors of his life.

This sprint along a street of squalid frame houses will be the beginning of something that will not cease until George has finally succeeded in running from the town itself. And when he does, his escape from Winesburg will be not merely a running away from, but a running toward, something—life, love, fame, adventure, anything, everything—that the town has (almost maliciously, it seems) denied him.

Elizabeth Willard dies of a paralytic stroke. Like her life, her death can only show itself as the paralysis so symbolic of all the paralyzed lives of this town. But if she has lived and died in one form of paralysis or another, her son George will at least act to break out of this grip on his life. Thus, with the death of his mother, George grows up in a hurry. For he is barely out of adolescence when Elizabeth dies, in the same month that George reaches his eighteenth birthday. But because there is still much of the boy in George, vestigial traces of innocence still cling to him. In spite of the experience he has undergone by this time, and in spite of Elizabeth Willard's death, George's innocence, though steadily diminishing, is still strong enough to act as a protective shield against the harsh facts of life and death. For though Willard is not exactly shocked by his mother's death, he finds it difficult to believe.

Not only can he not seem to realize the fact of that death but, even more significantly, he cannot seem to realize the fact of death itself. This death in the family is still too unreal to register fully upon his consciousness. George may appear to be too callously detached, but that state of mind is induced by the unreal reality of the situation rather than by his lack of sensitivity:

> The young man went into his own room and closed the door. He had a queer empty feeling in the region of his stomach. For a moment he sat staring at the floor and then jumping up went for a walk. Along the station platform he went, and around through residence streets past the high school building, thinking almost entirely of his own affairs. The notion of death could not get hold of him and he was in fact a little annoyed that his mother had died on that day. (pp. 280–81)

Although he is much older than the Nick Adams of Hemingway's "Indian Camp," George, like Nick, is unable to face the reality of death, or to see any reference or suggestion that one human being's death is only part of a recurrent pattern that foreshadows one's own death. Like Nick, George is still young enough to feel "quite sure that he would never die"—though that feeling will not last much longer. Thus, as yet unable to consciously accept the fact of death, George turns aside to seek some other answer. He must look forward to tomorrow, signifying life and rebirth, rather than back into yesterday, signifying death, literally and figuratively.

In the episode "Death," George decides to leave Winesburg; it is Elizabeth Willard's death that has impelled George to make that inevitable decision:

> Again [George] thought of his own affairs and definitely decided he would make a change in his life, that he would leave Winesburg. "I will go to some city. Perhaps I can get a job on

some newspaper," he thought and then his mind turned to the girl with whom he was to have spent this evening and again he was half angry at the turn of events that had prevented his going to her. (p. 282)

The last episode, "Departure," in which George takes his leave of the town, places him on the borderline of manhood, but not completely across it into full maturity. At this time, there lies within George the potentiality for a full—or fuller—maturity. When it comes, his departure is both the precondition and the end result of a process of initiation and maturation for which all of his previous life in the town had merely been preparation.

George's departure from the town is not only a rebirth but a burial of the old self. Yet the death here is never really a complete death of that old self; for the mixture of memory and desire will keep George tied to the past, no matter how delicate or tenuous the attachment may be. Nostalgia dies hard; and it is not the big things but the small events of daily life, the seemingly unimportant minutiae, that hold George captive in a way to the past, a young man "on parole," so to speak, from that past. The small, carelessly overlooked details will stand out now that George must take his leave of them.

He thought of little things—Turk Smallet wheeling boards through the main street of his town in the morning, a tall woman, beautifully gowned, who had once stayed over night at his father's hotel. Butch Wheeler the lamp lighter of Winesburg hurrying through the streets on a summer evening and holding a torch in his hand, Helen White standing by a window in the Winesburg post office and putting a stamp on an envelope.

The young man's mind was carried away by his growing passion for dreams. One looking at him would not have thought him particularly sharp. With the recollection of little things occupying his mind he closed his eyes and leaned back in the car seat. He stayed that way for a long time and when he aroused himself and again looked out of the car window the town of Winesburg had disappeared and his life there had become but a background on which to paint the dreams of his manhood. (p. 303)

Thus, in "Departure," we are given what amounts to George's first and last significant act in the context of the book—his departure from the town and the journey into the world that now awaits him.

Significantly, George Willard, like Theron Ware before him but not necessarily for similar reasons, leaves Winesburg on a spring morning one month after Elizabeth Willard's death, an action that more than suggests the vernal quality of this ritual of passage; for Willard is at not only the season of spring in the world but in his life. He leaves town, one might say, at the instance, or *instant*, of his mother's death, the better that he may be reborn into the new life that awaits him; for it is as a young man scarcely out of boyhood—in his eighteenth year—that George leaves Winesburg. It is also fitting that he should leave in the spring of his manhood and in the spring season; in both, metaphorically speaking, the season is one of the rebirth of hope, a feeling George is certainly filled with as the train pulls out of the Winesburg depot.

Like so many escapers in the modern American novel, Willard is a type who both looks backward to the escapers who have preceded him and ahead to those who will follow. Like George, these escapers—the Huck Finns, Theron Wares, Frederic Henrys, and John Andrewses—are generalized types, characteristic of so many escapers in American fiction. They are fleeing not merely a set of untenable circumstances (which all of them, in one way or another, do) but also something within their former selves that must be fled if they are to come to greater maturity. *En partant, nous mourons un peu*—in parting, we die a little; and the parting that George undertakes, like all such partings, indeed betokens a kind of death—not only of George's younger self but of the town he has left behind. Of course, in parting we also experience a rebirth of sorts too. Thus, his journey to the city is no simple geographical journey; it is a journey into life itself. Paradoxically, in spite of the suggestions of mutability and mortality in George's departure, the town begins to live again in his memories of it.

Willard's escape from Winesburg is, in short, a "revolt from the village," involving all the implications of that phrase; it is an escape from a petrified world and a present that has overnight become a dead past. With his departure from Winesburg, George has taken his first step into the future, and the town has, accordingly, taken its place in his past.

1. For a detailed study of the initiation theme, see Robert S. Bickham's "The Origins and Importance of the Initiation Story in Twentieth Century British and American Fiction," (Ph.D. diss., University of New Mexico, 1961).

2. "The stories [in *Winesburg*] belonged together. I felt that, taken together, they made something like a novel, a complete story . . . the feeling of the life of a boy growing into young manhood in a town" (Sherwood Anderson, *Memoirs,* p. 289).

3. From WINESBERG, OHIO by Sherwood Anderson, pp. 4–5. Copyright 1919 by B. W. Huebsch, renewed 1947 by Eleanor Copenhaven Anderson. Reprinted by permission of the Viking Press, Inc. All further quotations are taken from the 1958 edition.

4. Within the context of Winesburg, George is only relatively more articulate than his fellow townsmen. For in moments of high emotion, George's interior monologues tend to become a sequence of emotion-tinged pep-talks: his chronic need to take walks, when he cannot give a lucid answer to a difficult question ("Mother"), or the notion that he "must be orderly . . . must . . . get into touch with something orderly and big that swings through the night like a star" ("An Awakening").

chapter five

John Andrews:
Flight from the Machine

"God! if there were somewhere
nowadays where you could flee. . . ."
—Martin Howe,
One Man's Initiation—1917

In John Dos Passos's novel *One Man's Initiation—1917* (1920), the hero, in an outburst of anger and disgust at the tedium of his condition, blurts out: "God! if there were somewhere nowadays where you could flee. . . ." These words, uttered with such desperation, are not only appropriate in the mouth of Martin Howe—the prototype of John Andrews in *Three Soldiers* (1921)—or even of Andrews himself; the outburst might equally apply to the many heroes and antiheroes in the modern American novel who see no way out of their predicaments other than through escape, whether from war or the crushing machine of the industrial civilization that has produced it. But if John Andrews's predecessor voices such a sentiment, then John Andrews himself would not only voice the sentiment but act upon it. For the musician-artist hero of *Three Soldiers* will ultimately rebel against the regimentation of army life by deserting that life—only to be brought back finally into custody to stand trial for desertion; and though there seems to be a qualified heroism about the gesture, the effects of that heroism are nullified by the army "machine," along with the anarchic individualism that originally impelled the heroic gesture. In this first comparatively successful novel, Dos Passos—in the guise of the aesthetic John Andrews— seems to say that, no matter how admirable or justified the individual's effort to escape regimentation, the individual himself will ultimately be crushed by it. This seems to be both the message and the protest of the author who wrote *One Man's Initiation—1917,* a message of protest that, in one form or another, Dos Passos has sounded throughout all his works—the nonfiction equally with the fiction.

Three Soldiers is dominated by one obsessive theme, which affects not only its technique and structure but saturates its tone. This theme, of course, is the crushing regimentation of military life. The men who are part of this life are simply unthinking automatons that go to make up those interchangeable parts of the larger impersonal machine. Without the monotony, the drudgery, the tedium of army life in wartime—these are intensified when peace comes—Andrews's escape itself would be meaningless. Here, the escape is *not* an act of irresponsibility on the part of one individual toward his fellow men (though it may well be interpreted as that). Given Andrews's circumstances, it becomes almost obligatory; for it is not merely an act of impulse but a statement charged with the denial of all the values that the military mind—and in some instances its civilian counterpart—holds dear. In short, Andrews's escape is both a revolt and a statement of that revolt against the forces that would crush him.

The opening lines of *Three Soldiers* set the tone for the theme of the novel. Men are always lining up, exhausted from long hours of drilling and marching. A characteristic opening for a consistently large number of passages and chapters throughout the book might be: "The company stood at attention, each man looking straight before him at the empty parade ground. . . ." Or: "The company was lined up for morning mess." Or: "The men were lined up in the village street with their packs on, waiting for the order to move." These and similar opening scenes reappear almost as incremental repetitions for this essentially contrapuntal novel. And the repetition, like the pounding of marching feet or the monotonous strokes of arms washing barracks windows, itself comes to express something of the obsessive leitmotif that runs through the book. *Arbeit und Rhythmus* is the phrase that repeatedly imposes itself on Andrews's thoughts as he washes barracks windows. "*Arbeit und Rhythmus*" the world of the army seems to answer back, almost as though the rhythm of Andrews's life might be struck off by a monster (or monstrous) metronome. Significantly, the musical composition that Andrews will be working on at the time of his desertion—blown off the table, sheet by sheet, by a gust of wind—will be entitled "Soul and the Body of John Brown," a hymn to freedom. Even the Stateside army camp where the three soldiers Fuselli, Chrisfield, and Andrews are stationed resembles a prison. Fuselli, on his way out of camp on an overnight pass (that smaller, sanctioned form of escape), briefly notes the camp fences, "surmounted by three strands of barbed wire." [1] Yet the town toward which he directs his footsteps has little more to offer than the smaller "town" within the barbed wire enclosure.

Whatever the obsessions Fuselli and Chrisfield harbor (the ambition to be a corporal in the first; the urge to kill a bullying non-com in the second), it is Audrews's obsession that dominates *Three Soldiers*. His need to escape from the army has virtually become, even before he has gone overseas, an *idée fixe*. Regimentation is intolerable to Andrews (this is essentially the message of the novel). From the beginning he has had a low tolerance for restricting situations; and one can almost predict, given Andrews's character and predicament, his eventual desertion. The qualities are all there; yet Andrews's enlistment in the army, in the first place, is perhaps his first move toward a greater escape—from the larger industrial civilization that has threatened his selfhood. That he chooses the army to escape something that, by its very nature, can hardly be *worse* than army life, is one of the curious paradoxes of this work. For Andrews's escape *into* the army reveals his own innocence in the face of his subsequent initiation into the realities of army life.

Unlike the system of World War II, under which soldiers were discharged on the basis of an accumulation of earned service and combat points, the method of discharge in World War I seemed as arbitrary as it was haphazard. Duty in the Army of Occupation in Germany for an indefinite stay might easily have become—and, indeed, in some instances did become —the doughboy's fate. This was the predicament in which John Andrews and large numbers of his comrades-in-arms found themselves when the armistice was signed on November 11, 1918. Thus, it is not difficult to understand the feelings of near-hopelessness and futility that assailed them for, ironically, surviving the war. If they were going to survive the peace, then it would be up to each of them to make good his own escape— either through "chains" of command or, if necessary, through illegal manipulations. And so for John Andrews at the termination of hostilities,

> life would continue to be this slavery of unclean bodies packed together in places where the air had been breathed over and over, cogs in the great slow-moving Juggernaut of armies. What did it matter if the fighting had stopped? The armies would go on grinding out lives with lives, crushing flesh with flesh. Would he ever again stand free and solitary to live out joyous hours which would make up for all the boredom of the treadmill? He had no hope. His life would continue like this dingy, ill-smelling [railroad] waiting room where men in uniform slept in the fetid air until they should be ordered out to march or stand in motionless rows, endlessly, futilely, like toy soldiers a child has forgotten in an attic. (pp. 228–29)

Three Soldiers is the story not only of John Andrews but of Andrews's friends, Privates Fuselli and Chrisfield. These two share with Andrews the need to escape. But each harbors this need for quite different reasons: Chrisfield deserts after killing a non-commissioned officer who had continually bullied him; Fuselli contracts a venereal disease and, by default, "escapes" his own confrontation with combat; and John Andrews makes his own bid for freedom, though it is foredoomed from the beginning.

As early as the first chapter in *Three Soldiers,* there is already that foreshadowing of the theme that will run through the book. Fuselli, in identifying himself with a soldier who had punched an officer in the jaw and is now hunted by the military police, weaves a fantasy of empathy in the snug warmth of his barracks cot:

> How cold and frightful it must feel to be out of the camp with the guard looking for you! He pictured himself running breathless down a long street pursued by a company with guns, by officers whose eyes glinted cruelly like the pointed tips of bullets. . . . Somebody had said there'd be promotions soon. Oh, he wanted so hard to be promoted. It'd be so swell if he could write back to Mabe and tell her to address her letters to Corporal Dan Fuselli. (pp. 16–17)

Here, of course, Fuselli's escape fantasy is ambiguously composed of two halves of a reverie: he too would like to punch a supercilious lieutenant in the jaw, but he sees himself as a fugitive fleeing the security of army routine. Yet if he can stay in the army *and* get a promotion—another sanctioned form of escape—he will have achieved the best of both worlds. However, since Fuselli spends his time daydreaming rather than acting, his progress toward a greater freedom is inevitably doomed. Instead of fulfilling himself, either as a corporal (which he becomes for a short period) or as an escaper in the manner of Andrews and Chrisfield—a fulfillment of sorts, dubious as it is—Fuselli, by a series of declensions, descends from the medics into something called the "optical detachment," after which he is reassigned to a labor battalion for having contracted V.D. Permanent kitchen police will be his lot, a purgatory he will have to endure until the end of his enlistment.

Chrisfield, too, occasionally escapes through daydreams:

> He thought of the spring on the plains of Indiana and the mocking-bird singing in the moonlight among the flowering

locust trees behind the house. He could almost smell the heavy
sweetness of the locust blooms, as he used to smell them sitting
on the steps after supper, tired from a day's heavy plowing,
while the clatter of his mother's housework came from the
kitchen. He didn't wish he was back there, but it was pleasant
to think of it now and then, and how the yellow farmhouse
looked and the red barn where his father never had been able
to find time to paint the door, and the tumble-down cowshed
where the shingles were always coming off. (pp. 139–40)

Thus, Chrisfield's "escapes," up to his final desertion, are enacted through memory: the memory of his home back in In-
diana, the barn, the fields, and so on. Yet Chris eventually
does make good his escape when he later kills an NCO who had
constantly bullied him. Chrisfield's escape thus becomes a kind
of thematic paradigm for the novel, for it has only further
served to convince us that the urge to escape is not limited to
sensitive, aesthetic Harvard men like Andrews but, more pointedly, includes even semiliterate farm boys.

Yet it is John Andrews, perhaps the most important member
of the trio, who seems to come nearest to being a representative
escape-hero. He is not simply an escape-hero but a man who
possesses all of the essential characteristics of the Dos Passos
hero—the romantic rebel against regimentation, the sensitive
young artist-opponent of all repression. For in spite of its apparent concern with army life, *Three Soldiers* is only inciden-
tally a novel about World War I. One might even suggest the
subtitle "A Portrait of the Artist As a Young Soldier," for
the novel shows us a young musician-composer seeking refuge
from all that would cramp his creative powers both as artist
and as individual. Andrews thus becomes the symbol of the
artist forced to suppress his nature in the face of the regimented
life that would crush that nature. If we look back to Martin
Howe of *One Man's Initiation—1917,* Andrews is a step for-

ward from his predecessor of the earlier, less successful, attempt to depict the artist crushed by society. Like Martin Howe, John Andrews also yearns for a place to which one could flee. In Andrews's case, however, the artist in him does finally manage to break through the outer husk of the soldier, so that the artist as individual might make good his escape. Like Howe, Andrews dreams of finding a place of refuge from the things that would thwart his creative drives.

While recovering from his wound in a military hospital, Andrews spends most of his time reading. Characteristically, though he reads Flaubert, he does not read the realistic *Madame Bovary;* instead he prefers the aesthetic *The Temptation of St. Anthony,* with its lush prose and its idealization of history. Besides, where *Madame Bovary* would lead Andrews back into prosaic reality, perhaps forcing him to identify with Emma Bovary's flight from that reality, *The Temptation of St. Anthony* will prove a temporary, if synthetic, form of escape from his own brand of reality. Andrews, in a sense, is a bookish Lieutenant Henry, but unable to define (as Henry is able to) the split between principles and reality. Further, while the aesthetic Andrews is a yearner and a dreamer, Hemingway's hero, as we shall see in chapter 5, prefers not to dream or think but to act. When Andrews has his fantasies about leading his company into mutiny, he knows that, after all, his mood is made up largely of the stuff of rhetoric and fantasy. Dos Passos says of him: "His mind [would flood] itself with rhetoric that it might keep its sanity" (p. 241). Hemingway's hero, on the other hand, *must dismiss* all rhetoric from his mind, the better to retain his sanity. Furthermore, Andrews, in playing out the role of the antihero, paradoxically transforms himself into something of a hero—as do so many antiheroes; for his heroism lies in his will to fight the entire military machine, regardless of the odds against winning the battle.

Even though Dos Passos apparently intended *Three Soldiers* to be a story involving the adventures of all three main characters—Fuselli, Chrisfield, and Andrews—the novel eventually becomes John Andrews's story; and before we are halfway into the book, Andrews has become its pivotal character.

Since Andrews is apparently the most sensitive and articulate of the three soldiers, it would appear logical that he would be the "lens" through which a more focused view of the predicaments of all three might be seen. Andrews, by degrees, not only grows into the viewpoint character but gradually assumes the stature—and the burden—of the main character; for in his resemblance to Dos Passos himself, he seems most capable of presenting this struggle of man against the machine in its most articulate light. His futility is not merely that of the soldier-hero sensitive to the abuses of military life; his is the perceptive eye that can see life as an extension of the industrial civilization that partly promotes that futility, where men are "wind-swept atoms" carried along by forces greater than themselves.

There seem to be at least four, largely unconscious, steps that Andrews takes toward making his final escape. The first of these—paradox that it may appear to be—is his enlistment in the army in the first place. Like so many young men of his generation who joined ambulance units and Red Cross detachments in 1917–18, Andrews sees the army, and more fuzzily the war itself, as a Great Adventure. When he embarks on the troopship for France, he is still imbued with those Homeric legends acquired at the university: he will sail off to prove his mettle in the lists of manly courage. In the instance of Fuselli there is the ironically inverted (and perhaps inadvertent) Homeric parallel: Fuselli's girl, Mabe, back in San Francisco, is a drab Penelope, but a Penelope who, unlike her original, eventually *does* surrender to a home-front suitor.

But for Andrews, escape into the army proves to be no escape at all. He attempts to escape from the aesthetic confines of

Harvard into what he believes will be a more exciting life, but he is disillusioned when he recognizes that he has merely traded one dissatisfying existence for another. Subsequently he applies for transfer into the school detachment, which will enable him, after the war, to attend lectures at the Sorbonne: this is Andrews's second step in his progress toward his final escape. Even here, however, the school detachment proves something less than stimulating; and so Andrews—perhaps momentarily forgetting his status as a soldier—takes an unofficial leave to visit friends in the Paris suburbs. This might perhaps be considered Andrews's third step toward his final escape, another of those unofficial leaves that have all the earmarks of his true intentions: to rid himself completely of the military life. But thus far these are only gestures. It is while Andrews is enjoying his period of "truancy" from the school detachment that he is apprehended by the military police and thrown into a disciplinary labor battalion; from there he will make his fourth (and final) escape. If the first three steps toward his final escape are largely vague, unplanned, half-conscious efforts, the fourth and final one is not. His escape from the labor battalion is a conscious desertion from the army itself.

In the modern American novel of escape, the perennial symbols of that rebellious urge are frequently railroad stations and the trains that depart from them. We see such scenes running through American fiction either as sustained scenes or as quick glimpses (usually at the beginnings or endings of novels). Andrews on his way to Paris and the school detachment indulges in the following reverie:

He was thinking how all the epochs of his life seemed to have been marked out by railroad rides at night. . . . The gusts of cold night air when he opened the window and the faint whiffs of steam and coal gas that tingled in his nostrils excited him like a smile on a strange face seen for a moment in a crowded street.

He did not think of what he had left behind. He was straining his eyes eagerly through the darkness towards the vivid life he was going to live. . . . In six hours he would be in Paris. . . . Every mile the train carried him away from things past. (pp. 268–69)

For Andrews, however, Paris is a symbol of liberty in more ways than one. Besides its conventional libertarian and cultural connotations, Paris for Andrews stands for personal liberation. As the train enters the suburbs of the city, "Andrews felt a crazy buoyancy bubbling up in him. The rumbling clatter of the train wheels sang in his ears. He threw himself on his back on the dusty blue seat and kicked his heels in the air like a colt" (p. 270). Even the imagery here is heightened by the comparison with a colt set free, kicking the turf from his hind hoofs. When Andrews leaves his rifle and cartridge belt—symbols of servitude—behind on the train, he has, if prematurely, already said goodbye to the army, made his own separate peace with the life that the rifle and the cartridge belt represent. For though Andrews's new freedom is not a complete freedom from the army, it still has its own intoxicating effects on him. When the train arrives in Paris and Andrews alights, every nerve and fiber in his body is alert:

He was free now of the imaginings of his desire, to loll all day at café tables watching the tables move in changing patterns before him, to fill his mind and body with a reverberation of all the rhythms of men and women moving in the frieze of life before his eyes; no more like wooden automatons knowing only the motions of the drill manual, but supple and varied, full of force and tragedy. (p. 289)

Yet as Andrews will discover, his freedom is as illusory as it is short-lived, and the leash he is still attached to remains a leash whose length will only extend as far as army regulations will permit. But in the heady air of his new freedom, he forgets that he is still a soldier, subject to military regulations. The machine, though momentarily stilled, is ready to come alive when the need arises, to crush the troublesome particle between its cogs.

When Andrews does make his escape—initiating it with a plunge into the Seine River—he does so almost as a part of a dream rather than as a result of a planned action, even though the dreamlike manner of his escape is still part of his larger, consciously laid plans for it. Although he has often pondered over desertion, when he does finally desert, it comes almost as an act of momentary impulse, dictated ultimately by his earlier conscious planning—much like Huck's, in Twain's novel. In its impelling pressures it anticipates the escape that Lieutenant Henry will make when he plunges into the cold swift current of the Tagliamento in *A Farewell to Arms,* for whether it be the Seine in Andrews's instance or the Tagliamento in Lieutenant Henry's, the effects are identical in their ritualistic significance: the rivers serve as the means for the baptismal experiences of both Andrews and Henry. Further, like Henry, who changes into civilian clothes, John Andrews places the seal on his baptismal act by changing from his army uniform into the clothes of a bargeman, apparel conveniently furnished by a French barge family. Thus, literally and symbolically, Andrews has taken a plunge not only into the Seine but into another life; and the change of clothing most graphically represents the change in his career from soldier to civilian. Thus, the rebirth—represented by his change of clothing—is complete, short-lived as it is.

Yet even the abortive gesture of his escape, symbolized by the scattering of his pages of music by gusts of wind, will remain a gesture. For the reality that comes to John Andrews at the end of the novel negates the entire purpose of his escape, and he is returned to pay the penalty for that strong but unsanctioned impulse. Yet we cannot say that the negation is complete, since there is a residue of meaning in the gesture itself. Although Andrews is eventually recaptured and returned to his outfit, he has at least tasted freedom. No matter what the machine may do to him now, it will never again be able to take away his supreme moment of rebellion and his triumph in that moment; for Andrews's liberation, long before his recapture and return to his outfit, has been an inner liberation, a liberation of soul. Just before that recapture, he tells one of his fellow deserters: "It's funny, Al . . . I'm not a damn bit scared any more. I think I'm free of the army . . ." (p. 407).

Finally, before his recapture, in his talk with Genevieve Rod, his French girl friend, we get not only Andrews's credo but the belief that Dos Passos himself has held onto through the years of his own growth, a growth that transcended his own involvements in political causes of the moment:

> "It seems to me . . . that human society has been always that, and perhaps will be always that: organizations growing and stifling individuals, and individuals revolting hopelessly against them, and at last forming new societies to crush the old societies and becoming slaves again in their turn. . . ." (p. 421)

When John Andrews utters these words, we can hear another John talking—Dos Passos. Virtually until the day he died, Dos Passos continued to speak out against those "slave societies" no matter their shade or political complexion. And it was this that earned him and his work many detractors as well as admirers.

---

1. John Dos Passos, *Three Soldiers* (New York, 1921), p. 12. Copyright by H. Marston Smith and Elizabeth Dos Passos, co-executors of the estate of John R. Dos Passos, and used with their permission. All further quotations are from this edition.

chapter six

Frederic Henry:
The Run for Life

And we are here as on a darkling plain
Swept with confused alarms of struggle and flight,
Where ignorant armies clash by night.

Matthew Arnold,
"Dover Beach"

In Ernest Hemingway's *A Farewell to Arms* (1929), a book equally divided between two types of romance and one of stark reality, the hero, Frederic Henry, attempts to flee both the false romance and the stark reality which that romance camouflages. Yet the romance has another, more genuine level, that of Henry's love for Catherine Barkley, and serves to counterpoint the false romance of a "picturesque war" that is anything but picturesque; it is the harsh reality (of the war) rather than its fake romance that Lieutenant Henry eventually flees. Finally, when Henry himself is in danger of a senseless summary execution—part of the larger senselessness of the war—he plunges into the Tagliamento River, escapes the war, and, like John Andrews before him, makes his much celebrated "separate peace."

The split upon which Frederic Henry's escape from the war is predicated is that which exists between the realities of the war and its alleged glory. This romantic byplay is pointed up by the rhetoric employed to inspire whatever remnants there may be of inspiration within the apathetic and the cowardly. If we can believe T. E. Hulme, romance, or romanticism, is often given to an excess of rhetoric; and in *A Farewell to Arms* it is an attack on that excess that we encounter. It is the same sort of talk that John Andrews in *Three Soldiers* encounters in the Y-men, and it is the talk that is used to glorify all wars, whatever their justification. Between the realities of the war and the rhetoric lies the unambiguous shadow. Critics have frequently made this point in their analyses of Hemingway's novel, usually quoting the passage beginning with, "I was always embarrassed by the words sacred, glorious, and sacrifice and the expression in vain . . ." and ending with, "and I had seen nothing sacred, and the things that were glorious had no glory and the sacrifices were like the stockyards at Chicago if nothing was done with the meat except to bury it." [1]

This war, then, is not a war seen through the haze of a romantic past—flashing swords, cavalry charges, the *appearance* of high romance—but a new kind of war, where swords, those symbols of old wars, are outmoded both in fact and as symbol. We see this when Henry, returning to the front from a convalescent leave, goes into a shop to buy a pistol. "How much is this?" asks Henry of the woman shopkeeper, after which the following dialogue ensues:

> "Fifty lire. It is very cheap."
> "All right. I want two extra clips and a box of cartridges."
> She brought them from under the counter.
> "Have you any need for a sword?" she asked. "I have some used swords very cheap."
> "I'm going to the front," I said.
> "Oh, yes, then you won't need a sword," she said. (pp. 148–49)

Swords now are more valuable as ceremonial adjuncts than as practical weapons. Thus, without seeming to say very much, Hemingway manages with exceeding skill to communicate his point that not only are swords outmoded as weapons but are even ludicrous in this particular war. One does not need a sword to accomplish what machine guns or artillery can produce with greater—more deadly—efficiency. The shopkeeper's appeal to Henry, that her swords are both used and cheap, carries ironies beyond the point of the denotative reference of those words. Curiously, if one detaches the first letter of the word *sword,* one is left with *word;* and it is words that are now used (or overused) and that are also cheap. In this context Henry comes to distrust words. Plainly then, like the used and the cheap swords, used and cheap words no longer belong in a war that is far more real than the rhetoric woven around it.

So much for romance and rhetoric. But what of the realities? Again Hemingway pictures the specifics that act as vehicles for those realities. When Rinaldi, Henry's surgeon friend, visits Henry in the field hospital, he asks him certain pointed and leading questions about Henry's wound and the circumstances that led up to it:

> "Tell me exactly what happened. Did you do any heroic act?"
> "No," I said. "I was blown up while we were eating cheese."
> "Be serious. You must have done something heroic either before or after. Remember carefully."
> "I did not."
> "Didn't you carry anybody on your back? Gordini says you carried several people on your back but the medical major at the first post declares it is impossible. He had to sign the proposition for the citation."
> "I didn't carry anybody. I couldn't move." [2]
> "That doesn't matter," said Rinaldi. (p. 63)

That Henry is to receive the silver medal for a valorous act he did not carry out is additional irony to bring home the larger irony in the business of medal-awarding itself. For in this new war, carrying wounded to safety under fire, eating cheese while the shells scream in, or simply being part of a drunken artillery battery on the way up to the front (as portrayed in the inter-chapter in *In Our Time*)—*c'est tout égal:* it all works out to a silver medal.

In *A Farewell to Arms* a stark catalog of the attributes of modern warfare is presented. Early in the book, Rinaldi is talking to Henry, who has just returned from a leave: "Since you are gone [he tells Henry] we have nothing but frostbites, chilblains, jaundice, gonorrhea, self-inflicted wounds, pneumonia and hard and soft chancres. Every week someone gets wounded by rock fragments. There are a few real wounded . . ." (p.

12). Rinaldi is, of course, talking shop as a surgeon. Physical debilitation and deterioration prove good topics to relieve the boredom. Yet this dreary catalog of melancholy events seems to come closer to the truth about warfare than even the famous passage so often quoted, which involves the contrast between the rhetoric and the names of towns and rivers, the numbers of regiments. But it is finally in the setting of *A Farewell to Arms* —the chaos and the disorder of the retreat at Caporetto, so sharply contrasted with the "neat" little wars of the nineteenth century—that the disgust with twentieth-century reality is more forcefully shown.

In this novel of war, disillusionment, and subsequent escape from both, Lieutenant Frederic Henry is not only the central character but also the fictional and moral viewpoint of the story. As for Henry in terms of fictional reality, there are two Frederic Henrys—the early Tenente, before the retreat from Caporetto, and the Fredric (or *Mr.*) Henry subsequent to that (and his own) retreat. Between the two Henrys, or the two periods that form the boundaries of Henry's major action—his escape—lie all of those reasons and pressures and motivations that eventually bring about that escape.

The early Henry previous to Caporetto is an impassive young man who has already become partly inured to the world of pain and to some of the harsh realities beyond the war. For Henry has not exactly come to the war expecting only glory and adventure; his enlistment in an ambulance unit is not so much an act of false heroics or bravado as it is an escape from something presumably more objectionable than the war itself. We are not told much about Henry's past before his enlistment, other than that he has been studying architecture in Rome. What we know is that he is a young American who has volunteered for service in the ambulance corps; that he has, vaguely, some relatives back in the States who periodically send him money to supplement his meager lieutenant's pay. But this is all we know—providing, of course, one takes for granted an ignorance of Henry's fictional predecessor, Nick Adams. If Frederic Henry, as many critics see him, is the young Nick Adams grown slightly older, then Henry's joining the ambulance unit begins to appear more "logical" and even manages to fit into the large escape pattern of the novel. For Henry's escape into the Italian army—and it is an escape of sorts—can only be understood in the light of Hemingway's earlier work. As Francis Hackett has suggested, the escape into the Italian army is no mere act of bravado; it is an escape from other unpleasantnesses that a younger Frederic Henry—the earlier Nick Adams—has already experienced in the Michigan woods.[3]

The pre-Caporetto Henry, when he goes on leave, makes his absence from the front serve as a temporary escape. He had wanted to go to the Abruzzi mountain home of his friend the priest, "where the roads were frozen and hard as iron, where it was clear cold and dry . . . and the peasants took off their hats and called you Lord"; but instead he had gone down into the plains and the cities of those plains, each offering its own form of escape, the "smoke of cafés and nights when the room whirled and you needed to look at the wall to make it stop, nights in bed, drunk, when you knew that that was all there was . . ." (p. 13). Already, this early in the novel and in Henry's life as a soldier, the more splendorous illusions have been lost. But Henry is still not intent on making any meaningful escape, only a passive agreement with himself to stick things out before going off to the cities behind the lines to temporarily lose himself in drunkenness and forgetfulness.

As early as chapter 2, in the officers' billet, various proposals for more limited escapes are half-entertained, in the parodied manner of a Baedeker's guidebook. The major, a lieutenant, and the priest give their own social, spiritual, and geographical versions of this need to get away from the present reality of the war. The major states that all thinking men are atheists (the escape from God) ; but the major does not believe in the Freemasons either, who, for the priest, are no better than atheists. The lieutenant, on his part, believes the Freemasons to be a noble organization. They then both recommend that Henry visit their favorite towns and places when he goes on leave. The major feels that Henry should visit Rome, Naples, and Sicily. The lieutenant recommends Amalfi (ironically, that Websterian place of blood and revenge!), where "they will love you like a son." The priest would like to see Henry go up to the Abruzzi where he could visit the priest's family at Capracotta (a name phonetically similar to that other town associated with a greater escape, Caporetto). The others, however, laugh at the priest for making this suggestion. It is, of course, part of their more general priest-baiting designed to compensate for their own wish to escape what the priest stands for. What need is there to go to the Abruzzi when Henry might as well go to Naples to enjoy the girls? Here is a foreshadowing, shown in the lewd talk of the officers, of the deeper split between Henry and his fellow officers, and the direction the escape will later take. The suggestions reveal a split between those escapes leading only to a momentary gratification of the senses and the truer escape (or greater responsibility?) of the love for God as represented by the windswept, snowcapped mountains of the Abruzzi.

The officers, then, in contrast to the priest, offer Henry escapes that are essentially escapes from one's deeper self. Here, the meaning of the priest-baiting becomes pointed: the officers are suggesting to Henry escapes that are the antitheses of all that the priest stands for—something, perhaps, that they themselves, courageous men that they are, would like to run away from. The priest is thus a constant reminder of the alternative to the escapes they offer Henry.

By chapter 7 Henry is already beginning to feel separate, and separated, from the others; for a new element has entered the story—Catherine Barkley. Now the choice is no longer between the highly spiritualized love and dedication of the priest and the passion without love of the officers. There is a third choice: it is the love that has the best elements of both the first and the second. This sense of separation Henry already feels by chapter 8, when he has already met Catherine, and his interests have taken a new turn. At this stage, however, full and complete love has not yet developed; there is still only a kind of prurient curiosity, a willingness to make his relationship with Catherine a game of chess. Yet from the moment of his first meeting with her, Henry, without quite realizing it, has already taken the first tentative step toward making his separate peace. If billet camaraderie is part of the war, then Henry can only go through the motions instead of feeling emotion. He is already separate from the others, and as he tells us:

> "They [the officers and the priest] talked too much at the mess and I drank wine because tonight we were not all brothers unless I drank a little and talked with the priest about Archbishop Ireland. . . .
> "Half-way through the wine I did not want any more. I remembered where I was going." (pp. 38–40)

Rinaldi tells the others that Henry has a "rendezvous" with Catherine Barkley, whom the lieutenant in his near-drunken condition had almost forgotten. But when he rouses himself from his stupor, he remembers Catherine with a pang of conscience. Until now, he had treated his relationship with her as a game of chess, where you looked ahead to keep from being biologically checkmated—something much more difficult to escape from than the army. But by chapter 7 the biological trap (which involves Henry's conscience) has been sprung, and when he leaves the officers' mess, a great loneliness and emptiness comes over him. Unlike the others back in the mess, he can no longer look upon love as a dirty word; and when he almost misses seeing Catherine, a greater feeling of loss comes over him, foreshadowing the last loss at the novel's end: "I went out the door [of the billet] and suddenly I felt lonely and empty. I had treated seeing Catherine very lightly, I had gotten somewhat drunk and had nearly forgotten to come but when I could not see her there I was feeling lonely and hollow" (p. 41).

By chapter 9 Henry still accepts the war, but not necessarily for any patriotic reasons. As he tells the ambulance drivers who are opposed to the war and believe that Italy should get out of it, the war is a bad job, but still a job that needs to be done and gotten over with. " 'I believe we should get the war over,' I said. 'It would not finish it if one side stopped fighting. It would only be worse if we stopped fighting.' " The war, as Henry admits, is bad; but quitting will not make things better. And so "we must finish it" (pp. 49–50).

But, as the saying goes, the voraciousness of the war seems to increase by what it feeds upon: the more brutal and callous the atrocities, the less human do men at war become, so that the individual is no longer regarded as a human being but as a number, a "tenth man," to be taken out and shot as a warning to others that even a regiment's failure to advance can be made into an act of cowardice for any given individual in that regiment:

> "Were you there, Tenente [asks one of the ambulance drivers], when they wouldn't attack and they shot every tenth man?"
> "No."

"It is true. They lined them up afterward and took every tenth man. Carabinieri shot them." (pp. 48–49)

Thus, the senselessness and the brutality of the war continue, where the brutalities no longer even repel the sensibilities, but only make those who see them and who testify to them even more brutalized themselves. " 'Carabinieri,' said Passini [another driver] and spat on the floor."

The senselessness of the war becomes even more pointed as the retreat at Caporetto gives way to the utter disaster of a rout, and the Italian rear guard starts to fire on its own troops. By now organization has disintegrated to the extent that in the rain-soaked darkness one cannot tell Germans and Austrians from Italians. But if the retreat has collapsed into rout, that situation is not materially helped by the confusion of Italians firing on their own men. The stupidity and the chaos continue as the retreat progresses, but long before Caporetto, the war has been stalled, with the only changes being brought about by the replacement of the wounded, the dead, the exhausted, and the battle-fatigued with fresh troops, who in their turn are put through the same futile and bloody treadmill. Henry, who has some knowledge of military history, suggests at one point an answer to the general low morale of the troops. What is needed is a leader. Inescapably, such a leader would be Napoleon. In that earlier war, back in that archaic century, Napoleon, though lacking all of the advantages of modern communications systems, had still been able to get things done. In that other war, a Napoleon or a Marshal Ney, or in individual instances even soldiers from the ranks, might have been capable of some single act of heroism, even if only limited to one of modest dimensions.

In this present war there is no longer room for heroism, either at the top or at the bottom. War has become a machine-like affair with such vast organizational logistics—regiments, divisions, armies—that the individual *as* individual has simply got lost in the larger machinery of the war. One gets wounded not in a blazing charge but while eating macaroni and cheese. Even Stephen Crane's Henry Fleming was not placed in such an ironically demeaning position. Fleming, dishonored as he feels himself to be in the first half of *The Red Badge of Courage,* survives long enough to make his "glorious" charge, ironically ineffectual as that charge is. But when Lieutenant Henry runs away from the battle (or rout), he neither seeks nor has the opportunity to redeem himself; for Henry Fleming felt there was some point in redemption, but Frederic Henry saw military redemption as part of the general obscenity of war's vocabulary—"sacred, glorious, and sacrifice and the expression in vain." Like the name Henry itself, the values of Henry Fleming and Frederic Henry have become transposed in the latter halves of each of these novels.

With each step along the inglorious road of retreat, the less obvious becomes more obvious to Henry. And if the war were, indeed, to go on for another hundred years—he suggests it might well be another Hundred Years' War—and were to be prosecuted in its present manner, there would be little point in going on; and that becomes even more pointless when the Italian military police summarily begin to execute those in the retreat above the rank of major. It is only then that Henry can articulate to himself the justification of his own desertion. That he sees the situation in analogical terms is not so much to Henry's credit—though we have to credit him with some sort of insight that sees the loss of a battle in terms of the loss of stock in a department store fire. But he carries the comparison tellingly further:

You had lost your cars and your men as a floorwalker loses the stock of his department in a fire. There was, however, no insurance. You were out of it now. You had no more obligation. If they shot floorwalkers after a fire in the department store because they spoke with an accent they had always had, then certainly the floorwalkers would not be expected to return when the store opened again for business. They might seek other employment; if there was any other employment and the police did not get them. (p. 232)

Until now, Henry has succeeded in keeping these unpalatable facts from himself. Indeed, up until his wounding, his involvement in the war had been almost that of a passive bystander. But on the retreat at Caporetto—which eventually becomes Henry's retreat—Henry sees the truth concerning something that he has until now only suspected: war respects no uniform, no tongue, no common interests; it permits battle police to mete out death with the impartial detachment of those who themselves are not immediately threatened by death. And it further numbs the sensibilities of those already brutalized. Henry has learned, and is still learning, his lesson; but the larger rationalizations and justifications begin to make their way into his consciousness. Even at the moment of his escape from the battle police into the Tagliamento, there is still no *conscious* moral rationalizations for his act; only an ex post facto justification of it, in which moral justification plays little or no part. Henry's escape thus points to survival (much as Huck Finn's) rather than to moral rebellion.

After Caporetto and his plunge into the Tagliamento, Henry's separate peace is complete. As he tells himself on the floor of the flatcar carrying him away from the front to Maestre, "It was not my show any more." Even here, Henry has the detachment of one who, though he has already seceded from the "show," bears no ill will or bitterness toward those who have hurt him. There is no "antiwar" philosophy here. Henry now looks at the war from the point of view of one who has been

burned and no longer wishes to go near the attractively deceptive fires with the innocence he had previously brought to them.
Abstractly, one may well regard fire as dangerous, hardly to be
played with; and this is Henry's view of the war before his
escape from the battle police. Many of his illusions have already been eroded, but the fact does not hit home with quite
the impact until the final debilitating "burning" of Caporetto.
Thus, when Henry secedes, he does so on impulse, as an act
of survival. It is only on the train carrying him away from the
war that Henry can regard his former life with the detachment
of a stranger. As Malcolm Cowley has suggested, the Frederic
Henry who came out of the Tagliamento is no longer the same
person who had plunged into it.

Henry's escape moves on two levels, both in terms of immediate causes and consequences and in terms of philosophical
implications. At its immediate level his escape tells us that he
is through with the war. But at another level his escape has
greater philosophical ramifications: He is not only done with
the war, like John Andrews in *Three Soldiers* before him, "bap-
tizing" that severance by his plunge into a river; his act, as has
frequently been noted, has symbolic value, for in his desertion
Henry has cut himself off from a world that makes war possible.

His plunge into the Tagliamento, however, is more than a
physical act, or at a more exalted (and critical) level, a philosophical commitment: it has psychological and mythological implications. Certainly, the *tenente* who dives into the river is not
the same person who comes out of it, totally exhausted, on the
other bank. Henry has been—and again we must give the nod
to Malcolm Cowley here—reborn, and, of course, through his
rebirth has acquired a new identity. He is no longer Tenente
but someone who was called that at one time, someone with a
dead (or perhaps no) past, a present of some sort, yet also

someone with an uncertain future. When he goes to Stresa, the fact becomes clear that he is no longer the Tenente of the first half of the book. He now wears civilian clothes, borrowed from a friend, in which he does not feel altogether comfortable. The clothes, then, like the act that necessitated them, still chafe at Henry's conscience. He tells us:

> In civilian clothes I felt a masquerader. I had been in uniform a long time and I missed the feeling of being held by your clothes. The trousers felt very floppy. I had bought a ticket at Milan for Stresa. I had also bought a new hat. I could not wear Sim's hat but his clothes were fine. They smelled of tobacco and as I sat in the compartment and looked out the window the new hat felt very new and the clothes very old. I myself felt as sad as the wet Lombard country that was outside through the window. There were some aviators in the compartment who did not think much of me. They avoided looking at me and were very scornful of a civilian my age. I did not feel insulted. In the old days I would have insulted them and picked a fight. They got off at Gallarate and I was glad to be alone. I had the paper but I did not read it because I did not want to read about the war. I was going to forget the war. I had made a separate peace. I felt damned lonely and was glad when the train got to Stresa. (p. 243)

Although Henry has made his separate peace, the war is still too close for him to be able to throw it off as he might "a wet bathing suit." The pangs of conscience are still strong, and will later reappear. For if Henry, before Caporetto, cannot entirely reject the war intellectually, after Caporetto he is not completely able to make the break with it emotionally. Hence, he is unwilling to read the news about the war or, though such news is available, relive the disastrous retreat that is still going on, in which many of his comrades are still involved. Yet Henry's identity has undergone a change, for in that idyllic mountain time with Catherine above Montreux, the landlord of the chalet they are living in addresses Henry as *Mr.* Henry. Neither the landlord nor his wife suspects Henry's past, or his status of deserter. For them, there is no Tenente Henry, only Mr. Henry. But the acquisition of new—or reborn—identities is implicitly interwoven with the necessity of leaving older places for newer ones: one must leave former places in order to acquire new identities; and one must go to those places where no one knows the former self ("We did not know any one in Montreux" [p. 292]).

Like those escapers who have preceded him and those who come after—the Joads, Jake Blount in *The Heart is a Lonely Hunter,* Bigger Thomas in *Native Son*—Henry must light out whenever the necessity dictates, to the Territory, to Seattle, to the big city, to California, or the town up the road—anywhere but where one has already been. With the move, the mover acquires his new identity. And with the acquisition of that identity, the escape, even though not always as effective as the escaper would wish, has completed its circuit.

In this novel of love and war, Catherine Barkley represents the escape from war into love and into life. Henry's love for Catherine, though it might be treated as "autotelic," not only is an integral part of the pattern of escape but, by its very nature and the circumstances under which it takes place, serves to highlight the death and futility of the war itself; for in love there is at least the possibility of a renewal of life. And certainly by its very nature, even in the most hopeless periods of trial and flight, there is hope. The violence of the war only serves to point up the precious fragility of the love between Lieutenant Henry and nurse Catherine Barkley. Thus, though it might sound like a callous judgment, Henry's love for Catherine—in its initial stages at least—is another form of escape from the war's violence and sterility; more, it is a counterpart (or counterpoint) to that violence and sterility.

Even if the love story is preposterous and unconvincing, as has occasionally been suggested, it is still an integral (and integrated) part of the story; for without it the pattern of the novel in its total effect would make even less sense, and the insanity of the war would be greater because unrelieved. In the love between Catherine and Henry there is at least the implication that not all actions in a world gone mad are themselves insane; that the only act that does make sense in a world of "confused alarms of struggle and flight" is the act of love itself. In this sense Matthew Arnold's "Dover Beach" is as much a poetic statement of what *A Farewell to Arms* is about as is (or perhaps even more than is) "To His Coy Mistress," the poem by Andrew Marvell that Henry recites to Catherine.

Although Henry's escape is a microcosmic example of the larger escape (or retreat) of the Italian army, it is paradoxically the great escape of the novel; for in that escape both the larger escape—the Caporetto retreat—and the entire senselessness of the war itself are made concrete. Just as the larger escape represents panic on a mass scale, so Henry's smaller escape represents the powerful instinct for self-preservation. Thus, when Henry makes up his mind to flee, it is not so much his mind that determines his action as it is his instinct to survive. Instinct rather than reason is the impelling force here. Like Huck Finn and John Andrews—and for probably similar "instinctive" reasons—Henry makes his dash for a river and goes in "with a splash."

In this retreat from Caporetto, the Italian army sets the tone and the circumstances of Henry's escape, and perhaps even justifies it in the face of the ineptness with which the whole retreat is managed. Thus, the retreat from Caporetto takes on symbolic value in that it seems to suggest (like the retreat itself, which begins in order and ends in disorder) the *world's* retreat from order; and that flight in turn is transformed into one man's flight. Caporetto thus becomes the obligatory scene, as drama critics would put it, of *A Farewell to Arms*. And in this novel of escape, the larger escape more than matches, in the power of its movement and the vividness of its setting, Henry's escape, thus forming a backdrop worthy of it.

A number of critics have noted the resemblances between Lieutenant Henry and other heroic (or antiheroic) escapers in American fiction. Three that immediately come to mind are Henry Fleming (of Crane's *Red Badge of Courage*), Huckleberry Finn, and John Andrews; and it is the second two of this threesome who are in direct ancestry to Henry; for both Huck Finn and John Andrews, when they flee, do so for more than purely instinctual reasons. Behind their escapes lie those larger reasons—in Huck only semiconscious ones—that Fleming does not have, no matter how hard he tries to justify his flight. Both Huck's and Andrews's escapes have been dealt with at greater length elsewhere in this study. But the escapes and some of their attributes are sufficiently similar to Henry's for us to note one or two in passing. Both Huck and Henry encounter impasses when each resorts to prayer—and presumably come to a similar conclusion. In Huck's case it is explicit: prayer does not work; in Henry's case, though we do not share his thoughts, we can be fairly sure that his reaction is similar to Huck's. When Catherine is in the hospital and gives birth to a stillborn child, Henry frantically prays to God to keep Catherine alive. But she dies. Huck Finn also discovers that prayer, contrary to the Widow Douglas's allusion to "spiritual gifts," does not work for him either. The prayers of neither of these escapers work, and pragmatically, therefore—explicitly with Huck, implicitly with Henry—they are worthless; one survives (or does not survive) in spite of prayers. Prayers, then, simply become one more set of outmoded rituals in a rejected social order of unworkable ritual, an order from which both Huck and Henry are trying to escape. Perhaps, in escape, the purblind doomsters may be avoided after all—perhaps!

The similarity between Henry and John Andrews of Dos Passos's novel lies in the somewhat more tangible device the authors resort to in having their heroes divest themselves of their uniforms, a kind of ritual of rejection in itself. Henry, like Andrews, must also abandon his uniform in order to make his escape more effective; but the casting-off of the uniform implies not only a practical need but a symbolic rejection of all that uniforms (both their own and uniforms generally) have come to represent. The practical need is the necessary one of course: to get rid of something that would plainly mark them as deserters. But the symbolic implication is wider, though equally obvious; for discarding the uniform proves to be, both for Andrews and for Henry, a symbolic representation of the loss of the old identity and the gaining of a new one. It is the outer sign of the inner-established "separate peace."

Finally, we must ask one question concerning the larger meaning of Henry's escape: how successful has it been? We can answer this question only if we see Henry's attempt as something tied in with the larger tragic implication of being mortal, something that generally holds for virtually all of the escapers dealt with in this study. Frederic Henry has attempted to escape from war and from death into what he hopes will be—and is, to some extent—a way of love and life; but in spite of this hope, he will discover in Catherine Barkley's death the truth that one may run toward life and love, even partly succeeding in the attempt, but one cannot run away from death. Thus, when Henry concludes that "they" would kill you if "they caught you off base," this is not only Henry's conclusion but the conclusion that *A Farewell to Arms* inexorably leads to—as story and as the concluding principle of that story.

1. Ernest Hemingway, *A Farewell to Arms* (New York, 1929, 1957), pp. 184–85. All further quotations are taken from this edition. Quotations from the works of Ernest Hemingway are fully protected by United States and International Copyright. Used by permission of Charles Scribner's Sons.

2. This is, of course, a deliberate understatement on Hemingway's part (if for nonliterary purposes we equate Henry with Hemingway) and contains its own pointed undertones. For Henry's wounding is based on an actual incident at Fossalta di Piave, when Hemingway indeed carried a wounded soldier, under fire, to safety. For his "pains," Hemingway ran into machine-gun crossfire, in which some bullets pierced his legs. Like Lieutenant Henry, Hemingway was later decorated by the Italian government for heroism under fire. There is, of course, a touch of the hilariously absurd in this exchange between Henry and Rinaldi—especially as presented in the dead-pan manner of the passage. This, however, only heightens the irony of the wished-for glory (unselfish as Rinaldi thinks it is) and Henry's rejection of it.

3. "Hemingway: 'A Farewell to Arms,'" *Saturday Review of Literature,* 6 August 1949, pp. 32–33.

chapter seven

The Joads:
Flight into the Social Soul

"Highway 66 . . . is the
path of a people in flight. . . ."

From as far back as *Cup of Gold* (1929) to his most recent work, John Steinbeck has shown a proclivity for dealing with people who are searching for a golden land of happiness, the fulfillment of a dream, quests that of course entail an escape both into and away from the past. Indeed, the past in the novels of Steinbeck constantly forms the design not only of rare exotic moments but of those more mundane periods in the daily lives of his people, who are tied to those earlier times that produced them and that gave birth to what has come to be called the American Dream.

Like that first modern American novel of escape, *Adventures of Huckleberry Finn, The Grapes of Wrath* (1939) is not only a book of travel but a novel of escape—as in Tom Joad's instance, from the consequences of his acts; as in the instance of the Joad family, from the conditions and economics of the land; as in the instance of Preacher Casy, from an untenable past with its irreconcilable split between what the preacher is (or becomes) and the tenets he has long preached but now no longer believes in. If Tom Joad is the hero of this novel of escape, he is a hero who shares the characteristics of countless picaresque heroes who so often seem to be fleeing from something that threatens their well-being. But if he shares something of the tradition of the picaresque hero, he shares that tradition with the comic overtones omitted.

As in so many escape novels, *The Grapes of Wrath,* early in the book, includes a passage that foreshadows the escapes that are to come and that will set the tone for the book itself. We are given this suggestion in Preacher Casy's words about that ever recurrent and symbolic turtle: "The preacher nodded his head slowly. 'Every kid got a turtle some time or other. Nobody can't keep a turtle though. They work at it and work at it, and at last one day they get out and away they go—off somewheres.' " [1]

There are a number of escapers in *The Grapes of Wrath,* ranging from the turtle at a rudimentary level—which Casy uses as an example to illustrate his own condition—to such disparate individuals as Noah, Tom's retarded brother; Uncle John, his guilt-stricken uncle; and Connie Rivers, his weak-kneed brother-in-law. Since this is so, it would be well to point out that although these escapers have one thing in common— the urge to flee their predicaments—the reasons for their flights, and the way they make them, must be clearly distinguished.[2]

The first of the escapers is, of course, Tom Joad, both in importance for the structure of the novel and for the symbolic implications Steinbeck vested in him; for Tom, like so many escapers in the novel of escape, has the ability to rebound from defeat, to be reborn into a new, if still far from whole, man. Tom's status as an escaper is thus twofold: he is fleeing from the law (the breaking of his parole), and he is fleeing Oklahoma. But both are incidental in Tom, for when he decides to join his family in their flight from Oklahoma, he himself is under no obligation to flee anywhere; it is only because his family is going, and because of his strong family identification, that Tom decides to go along with them. Certainly there is nothing left for him in Oklahoma. Thus, though he is a breaker of parole, and therefore a fugitive, Tom is not so much running away from his status of parolee as ignoring it. Nevertheless, regardless of his reasons for leaving Oklahoma, he is still a fugitive from the law.

The two homicides—both of which Tom perpetrates if not instigates—are the precipitating causes of Tom's later predicaments and the flights that grow out of them. The first homicide takes place during a brawl: Tom is set upon by a drunken man for an imagined slight to the latter's sense of honor, whereupon Tom kills the man in self-defense. Thus, the first killing has no larger significance than the drunken brawl out of which it grew.

What, however, does seem of significance is that there is no conscious malice on Tom's part. It is simply a fight, though of course a fight that leads to a killing and its consequences. Tom, in his explanation to the preacher, tells how it all happened:

> We was drunk . . . at a dance. I don' know how she started. An' then I felt that knife go in me, an' that sobered me up. Fust thing I see is Herb comin' for me again with his knife. They was this here shovel leanin' against the schoolhouse, so I grabbed it an' smacked 'im over the head. I never had nothing against Herb. He was a nice fella. Come a-bullin' after . . . Rosasharn when he was a little fella. No, I liked Herb. (pp. 72–73)

The brawl and the killing that comes of it are almost casual in their lack of deadly intentions; indeed, as we see, Tom had actually liked his assailant. What he had done, though hardly to be condoned or justified except as an act of self-defense, was one of those actions that are either to be understood and forgiven or unqualifiedly condemned out of hand. Yet for Tom there is no sense of guilt; and even though he crows a little about the deed, there is little joy either.

His second homicide is the killing of a California deputy for having, in his turn, brutally slain the nonviolent Casy. Tom, like the biblical Moses—who also killed to avenge another injustice—has no more compunction about his act than Moses presumably had when he slew one of Pharaoh's taskmasters.[3] Like Moses, Tom experiences no sense of guilt but only the urge to flee those who would prosecute him; and though he does not try very hard to justify the act, he had felt no worse at the time (as he later tells Ma Joad) than "if he [had] killed a skunk" (p. 545). Thus, in both instances, Tom is able to justify —morally, if not legally—his acts while still retaining a clear conscience. Curiously, in both killings Tom uses a tool of labor to commit the acts. It is almost as if, lacking the opportunity for constructive labor in that time of depression, Tom finds himself using tools as murder weapons. Thus, by implication, the "dignity of labor" is grotesquely parodied when the implements of that "dignity" become the weapons of human indignity.

Tom's second escape contains within it the need to leave behind a past that has led to his plight. In the first escape there is no such intention, for he returns to his family, ready to take up his life as he had lived it before going to prison. But after he kills the California deputy, Tom must escape into a completely different way of life. If the first killing had come about because of Tom's instinct for self-preservation, the second had been precipitated by an angry impulse of the moment; thus, there is less justification—in the eyes of the law at least—for this second killing. If Tom is caught and found guilty by a court of law, as is likely, his chances of getting off lightly on the second occasion are virtually nil. Ma Joad's role in Tom's flight is to recognize this probability; even perhaps more than Tom himself she sees the necessity for his escape. In this sense she becomes the vatic mother figure oracularly telling Tom what he *must* do as opposed to what he ought to do: "You got to go away, Tom. . . ."

The outcome of Tom's escape is what I have preferred to call the flight into the social soul. When Tom leaves on this second flight, he leaves as a reborn individual who has taken on a new identity; he is no longer the Tom Joad who had stepped out of a penitentiary in Oklahoma, nor is he the Tom Joad of the trek to California, who merely believes that the way to get by is to put down one foot at a time. Tom has seen two ways of life: the first, that of the road and the Hoovervilles; the second, the government-operated camps, where cooperation rather than the struggle for existence is a way of life. He has thus been initiated into the knowledge of greater possibilities for himself and his people. When Tom avenges Casy's death, the events subsequent to his escape have an initiatory effect on him; and when after the killing of the deputy he climbs out on the other side of the stream, across which he has fled, Tom is no longer the man he was before his encounter with the deputy. Like those escapers by water before him, he emerges from the "baptismal" immersion a newborn man, who now realizes that he must take up the struggle where Casy had fallen.

Tom Joad's personality thus undergoes an evolution (or change) brought on by the kind of education he has received at the hands of society—most specifically, at the hands of the deputies who for him represent that society. His resentment, rooted at first in the material and the personal, expands later into the larger, slower-burning, more sustained indignation that grows out of the greater injustices his people suffer. If his first transgression—the murder of a man in a drunken brawl—has no large significance, the second (the murder of the deputy) has about it, if murder can ever be justified, something of a "higher law." For Tom has committed himself to the cause of another human being; he has avenged Preacher Casy, who has come to embody everything Tom has begun to respect.

Our view of Tom is that of a man in flight: as a parole violator from an Oklahoma penitentiary in the first instance, and as a fugitive from California law in the second. Yet escaper though he is, Tom's flight toward the end of the novel is no longer a blind flight born out of desperation and panic alone; his flight now has a purpose larger than the flight itself. For, paradoxically, escape leads him directly back into the larger society of the social soul (as distinct from the oversoul),[4] to all those who belong to the fraternity of the damned and the oppressed, in which the words "dignity of labor" have become empty and ritualistic, and where the demand, or even the request, for a living wage has become synonymous with the words "dirty red." Out of this education comes Tom's credo in the form of an answer to his mother's concern for his safety and the ultimate destination of his flight: "I'll be all aroun' in the dark. I'll be ever'where—wherever you look. Wherever they's a fight so hungry people can eat, I'll be there" (p. 572).

Perhaps the second most important escaper in *The Grapes of Wrath* is the ex-preacher Casy. We have already suggested that one reason for his desertion of gospel-preaching was his inability to reconcile his urges as a sensual man with his other-worldly preachments. Resolving that dilemma would have made a hypocrite of him. Thus, for Casy, the alternative is to accept himself for what he is and, indeed, even proclaim its rightness.

Casy's pilgrimages away from society and the decisions that come of them—unknown to Casy at the time—set in motion those events that not only will involve Casy, but will draw Tom Joad along with them too. As a foreshadowing of this eventuality, early in the novel Casy makes known his desire to accompany the Joads on their trek west: "The preacher . . . stood looking into the coals. He said slowly, 'Yeah, I'm goin' with you. An' when your folks start out on the road I'm goin' with them. An' where folks are on the road, I'm gonna be with them'" (p. 77). The statement foreshadows Tom's credo expressed to his mother at the end of the novel, perhaps even influencing the attitude that inspires that credo. Noteworthy is the switch from the more personal *"your* folks" (my italics) to the more generalized "folks," for Casy has begun to see himself as responsible not only to the Joads but to all people everywhere in flight. In spite of those intentions, however, the Joads still see Casy in his role as preacher, still expect him to say a grace at meals and preside at burials, as on the occasion of Grampa's death. If Casy no longer considers himself a preacher, he has yet to convince the Joads. Thus, spiritually, he is as necessary to them in spite of his transformation (or transfiguration) as they are to him because of it. And when the Joads make their exodus from Oklahoma, the preacher, like Tom, has nothing left to stay for either. Now the parched wasteland of Oklahoma symbolizes for him the arid doctrines he had preached for so long in that land. Thus, no longer having a purpose or a place on that land, Casy joins the family on their trek to California.

The Joads, then, continue to look to the preacher for moral sustenance on their pilgrims' progress toward a better life; for them, Casy plays the role of an articulate liberator. Of course, his idea of liberation is not limited merely to a physical escape from the old life; it embraces a new spiritual comprehension. Yet his is no purely philosophical liberation either, but a liberation of the soul *through* the body, through the good things of this life. In this sense Casy is still, in spite of his intentions to the contrary, the spiritual guide of the Joads and their community. Above all else, Casy is the articulate member of the group; he is not only a Christ figure (as many have suggested) but an Aaron, playing the articulate brother to Tom's impetuous Moses.

As liberator and spokesman Casy is able to make the first conscious and articulate appraisal of the larger migrant flight into the West:

> Casy said, "I been walkin' aroun' in the country. Ever'body's askin' that. What we comin' to? Seems to me we don't never come to nothin'. Always on the way. Always goin' and goin'. Why don't folks think about that? They's movement now. People moving. We know why, an' we know how. Movin' 'cause they got to. That's why folks always move. Movin' 'cause they want somepin better'n what they got. An' that's the on'y way they'll ever git it." (p. 173)

The utterance, of course, could fit any number of escape situations, whether in life or in the novel that attempts to portray that life; it might itself be the statement or the central idea of this study: "That's why folks always move. Movin' 'cause they want somepin better'n what they got." However, these statements of Casy are not blurted out in moments of impulse; they have been simmering in him for a long time. When he finally utters them, he does so as a result of the changes that have long been taking place within him. In the months before we come upon him, he had been absorbed in his own spiritual growing pains, though few traditional conservative Christian creeds would possibly care to apply the word *spiritual* to what Casy had been experiencing. Although it is not my intention here to stress the transcendental element in Casy's growth—quite the contrary!—there does seem to be a trace of the inner light in Casy's drift away from the old religion, an Emersonian renunciation, if one wishes, of the former doctrine, though nowhere is the suggestion made that Casy has renounced his old *un*Emersonian joys of the flesh.

Casy's escape is primarily an escape from his past, from what he was—spiritual rather than (as in so many escapes) primarily geographical. Yet it is not an escape merely from the older religious dispensations, or from the soul into the oversoul, as some critics have suggested; it is into something more down-to-earth. Although it is true that Casy uses the transcendental terminology (unwittingly, of course, and with Steinbeck furnishing the lines in the wings), and though it is possible that he may even vaguely sense some extramaterial significance in the words, he is, for the most part, in this world; and his actions, if they can be called religious at all, spring from the same motivations as those of Abou Ben Adhem, the man who loved God best because he loved his fellow man.

In contradistinction to what has so often been stressed, Casy's escape is primarily an escape into the *social* soul rather than into the oversoul. I do not mean to suggest that transcendental implications ought to be brushed aside—especially in Casy's growth as distinct from Tom's, where both are assumed to have experienced, in a greater or lesser degree, a "transcendental" transformation; what I do suggest—and I wish to sustain the distinction—is that Casy's drift away from the old religion is perhaps due as much to a change in his social consciousness as it is to an expansion of his human into a cosmic consciousness. Casy, at the request of the Joads, respectfully fulfills his old role as preacher by saying grace at meals. But he uses one occasion as an opportunity to speak of the inner change he has undergone:

> Nighttime I'd lay on my back an' look up at the stars; morning I'd set an' watch the sun come up; midday I'd look out from a hill at the rollin' dry country; evening I'd foller the sun down. Sometimes I'd pray like I always done. On'y I couldn't figure what I was prayin' to or for. There was the hills, an' there was me, an' we wasn't separate no more. We was one thing. An' that one thing was holy. (p. 110)

This passage, suggesting Casy's transfiguration as a transcendental phenomenon—before and after his death—has been frequently alluded to, to prove that transfiguration. But if illumination it was, it was an illumination that led Casy directly *from* the oversoul into the social soul. And though the passage has often been cited, another passage that follows quickly upon it and still forms a part of Casy's story has often been slighted, or perhaps unintentionally neglected. It is a passage that shows that Casy's view of the world was not limited to any abstract sense of oneness with a cosmos, whether metaphysical or social, but rather extended into a roughhewn, but nonetheless real, ethos of love:

> An' I got thinkin', on'y it wasn't thinkin', it was deeper down than thinkin'. I got thinkin' how we was holy when we was one

thing, an' mankin' was holy when it was one thing. An' it on'y got unholy when one mis'able little fella got the bit in his teeth an' run off his own way, kickin' an' draggin' an' fightin'. Fella like that bust the holiness. But when they're all workin' together, not one fella for another fella, but one fella kind of harnessed to the whole shebang—that's right, that's holy. An' then I got thinkin' I don't even know what I mean by holy. . . . I can't say no grace like I use' ta say. I'm glad of the holiness of breakfast. I'm glad there's love here. That's all. (pp. 110–11)

The third escaper in this novel of collective escape is Uncle John. As we have already indicated, Uncle John wishes to escape from a bad conscience. Like Tom, Ma, Pa Joad, and the preacher, Uncle John is attempting to make his own break with the past. Tom's break is from his status as ex-convict; the preacher's, from his former calling. But even when Uncle John as a guilt-laden supernumerary accompanies the Joads on their trek west, he is still the victim of his relentless guilts; to run from them, Uncle John escapes into drink. But drinking is ineffective as escape, since drunkenness only seems to intensify his guilts. The issueless result of his late wife's pregnancy, interestingly enough, foreshadows in its barren outcome the sterility of the land itself—that erosion brought on by a similar nonmalicious mistreatment that the pregnant woman had experienced; and Rose of Sharon's stillbirth later on is also brought on by the hard times that she experiences in sharing the general hardships of the Joads themselves. In its own way it is as certain and symbolic an outcome of the escape from sterility as was Catherine Barkley's misfortune in Hemingway's *A Farewell to Arms*. Sterility is not only a part of the eroded land; it becomes part of the lives of the people of that land, physically and spiritually.

Connie Rivers, Rose of Sharon's young husband, is unable

to stand the apparent hopelessness of the Joad's plight, to which he sees himself tied; at the first opportunity, he deserts his wife. Perhaps in another time Connie might have succeeded in withstanding the stress of the westward trek; but now, in this fourth depression-ridden decade of the twentieth century, the values of the Westward Movement—that high optimism and the vigor of a country in its youth—seem to have fallen into desuetude. Connie, however, in reneging on his responsibilities, does not stay put, but continues to move on. Since he cannot go back, he goes forward; it does not matter where, so long as it is away from responsibility. Unlike his westering predecessors of a previous generation, he is neither staunch nor determined. If there is a trace of determination in Connie, it is the determination to get as far away as possible from Rose of Sharon and her people. In this he shows up in strong contrast to the pioneer husbands (at least to the legendary picture we have of them) who, for the most part, were supposed to have stuck by their womenfolk and protected them. In pioneer times the family was presumably a more cohesive unit, if for no other reason than common protection. Even the squatter Ishmael Bush in Cooper's novel *The Prairie,* reprobate though he is, possesses a deep loyalty to his family. Indeed, as its head, he rules it with an iron hand. But if Ishmael Bush is a cross between the stern biblical patriarch and the pioneer father, what a falling-off there has been for the fathers of twentieth-century migrants! In this later time the men are either weaklings who desert their wives, like Connie Rivers, or, like the uprooted Pa Joad, fathers who must play a secondary role. It is Ma Joad who assumes the leadership of, and becomes the moral goad for, the family. Where, in an earlier time, the menfolk had led, now the women take over the guidance and running of the family; yet ironically they do so at a time when the family itself has begun to disintegrate. The disintegration had already begun, of course, when Grampa Joad had died before the family was out of Oklahoma.

Yet who is to say that Connie is not the one (comparative) realist among the entire family? The others trust in handbills telling of nonexistent work in California, but Connie has never believed in them. Even after the Joads are told that the handbills lie, they still push west, desperately, doggedly, hoping that the truth itself may turn out to be a lie.

In contrast to the optimism and self-reliance of an earlier generation, Connie has already lost the optimism, if not the self-reliance that was supposed to inspire it. If there is any self-reliance left in him—and there must be some, for he has cut his moorings to the group to fend for himself—it is the element of self-reliance transmuted into the baser metal of social Darwinism: each for himself and the devil take the hindmost! Connie's act is an act of desperation (as are those of all the escapers). Perhaps the logical end of self-reliance, then (as represented by Connie—or by John Andrews and Frederic Henry before him), is the defeat of hope, when the self is no longer capable of accomplishing tasks only masses of men can presumably better succeed in bringing about. For the turbid currents of the 1930s were bringing sweeping changes that, although they certainly included and affected the individual, nevertheless carried him along on those more powerful currents that were ultimately heedless of him or his struggles. Against hostile Indians, arid wildernesses, even starvation and sickness, one might put up a fight—providing that the bright hope could be sustained and could justify the suffering. But without hope, the hunger, the tedium, the hardships of the road, the hostility of townsfolk and deputy sheriffs—these finally cannot be endured. Thus, with the old hope gone, the newer pessimism lies up ahead, a dark cloud threatening storm.

I should now like to turn to the Joads' flight west as a collective phenomenon. First, it must be stressed that the immediate causes of their flight do not lie in volition but in circumstances over which the Joads, individually or collectively, have little or no control. Thus, although in a loose sense the Joads happen to be in flight from the conditions that have forced them from the land, they are not so much escaping from the land as they are *driven* from it. To all intents and purposes, their exodus has about it all of the essential elements of flight—so much so that (to allude to the biblical parallelism again) their flight has frequently been compared with that of the ancient Israelites from Egypt. (Even in their hurry to leave Oklahoma—the hasty preparations—there is the similarity to the earlier Exodus.) Thus, the central postulate concerning the Joads' escape is that it is not quite like that of any other escape dealt with here. Virtually every escaper discussed thus far has in some way been held in the grip of a motive strong enough to want to escape, even though these motives have frequently been the result of great pressures on him. This is the most important difference between the motives of the Joads and those of other escapers. In the others, one senses a strong desire to be off—to anywhere but where they happen to be: Huck, aboard his raft or into the Territory; Theron Ware, to Seattle; George Willard, to the big city. However, in the Joads there is almost a sense of nostalgia for the land that has served them as home for generations. For the Joads differ distinctly from the other escapers in that, for the most part, when the time comes for them to leave, *they do not want to go;* this cannot be stressed enough. They are forced off the land by the banks and the large farming interests, which can farm the land much more cheaply and efficiently than individual tenant farmers; the Joads are therefore forced to take to the road by such circumstances as drought, erosion, the obliteration of the individual farm, and the expulsion of the individual tenant farmer in order to make room for the larger combines. The only escaper in the conventional sense (in which escape has most frequently been discussed here) is Tom Joad. But even Tom goes along with the family because there is nothing left for him to do.

But whether the Joads are driven from the land or flee it, the effect upon them is still the same; they become refugees. The exodus is not merely from the land but from the conditions that have made the land what it has become—a wasteland. "And now they were in flight from the sun and the drought" (pp. 274–75). Sun and drought are, of course, two apparently indispensable conditions under which wastelands so often "flourish," and which make for both physical and spiritual aridity. The escape, or flight, as it indeed becomes once the Joads are on the road (for there is no turning back now should they wish it) is thus not voluntary but forced upon them.

The Joads not only learn what it means to be fugitives—in flight from a set of circumstances beyond their control—but, like Huck Finn, they learn to become the protectors of fugitives in flight from more specific and imminent dangers. In their departure from the Hooper ranch, in California, they conceal Tom (now a hunted man because he has killed a deputy) in the rear of the truck, between mattresses. Thus, the Joads, in the eyes of the law, become accessories to Tom's act, for they have knowingly concealed a murderer. When they leave the Hooper ranch to head north, they too are caught up in Tom's predicament, for they are helping him to make good his escape; they compound their participation in Tom's crime by concealing the criminal. These are the facts, whether the crime be morally justified or not. The Joads, together with Tom, now find themselves outside, if not opposed to, the law; and here is a paradoxical, though significant, instance of family loyalty in a novel that depicts families *and* loyalties in the process of breaking up in favor of the larger "family" (the migrants) and its larger loyalties. The flight of the Joads from the Hooper ranch therefore takes on, in all of its tensions, the qualities of Tom's flight from vigilante "justice" as well as from the more general, though nonetheless pernicious, evils of the society buttressing that justice. Thus, when Tom strikes the blow, he strikes it not for Casy alone, nor even for himself, but for the Joads and people like them.

Apart from their concerns for Tom, there are other ramifications in the Joad flight from the Hooper ranch. For them, the ranch has become, like Oklahoma before it, another Egypt. Tom, like Moses, has murdered an oppressor. But beyond, their exodus from the ranch lies partly in its intolerable conditions—the low wages, the hovels they live in, and the chronic strike-breaking warfare; thus the exodus from the Hooper ranch becomes a repetition of the exodus from the country around Sallisaw, Oklahoma. By the time the Joads have been rousted from the Hoovervilles that are continually threatened with arson by irate townfolk, or take their leave from the Hooper ranch, flight has become a chronic way of life for them. They are forever forced—either by people or by drought, flood, and hunger —to flee from one place to another, always on the move, always searching for a way out of their plight. Eventually, the westward flight of the Joads turns inward upon itself; and after their arrival in California, it is no longer a flight west but simply a flight, chronic and labyrinthine, down the road, to the next government camp, to another ranch, to a hundred and one dead ends of hope. The flight of the Joads thus becomes a chronic mode of existence.

The further west the migrants flee, the more they undergo a change of character. "They were not farm men any more, but

migrant men" (p. 267). This may partly explain the transformation in the roles of the men and the women, as in the case
of Ma and Pa Joad; immemorially farm life has been the life
of the patriarchal society. Now, uprooted, homeless, the basic
social unit—the family—has disintegrated; and with its disintegration, the values by which the family has lived have disintegrated. It is not simply an isolated family here and there
that seems to be on the move; it is virtually an entire country—
or at least a social stratum of that country. The flight of the
migrants westward is like a huge and disastrous military retreat; but unlike a retreat in conventional warfare, what lies
away from the battle zone may be even more disastrous than
what lies behind, in it.

I trust that it is now clear why I have preferred to speak of
the oversoul, which certain critics have attached to the feelings
of Tom and Casy, as the social soul. Yet, if what Tom and
Casy experience is an escape into the oversoul—"Maybe all
men got one big soul ever'body's a part of"—it is an escape
revamped to fit the social predicament of their time. For if the
Emersonian oversoul has at last come down to earth, it has
come transformed into the social soul, where the individual no
longer tries to become part of the larger, more nebulous (and
mysterious) cosmos, but now attempts to become a part of the
more familiar human cosmos—the society of his fellow men.

Spiritual salvation alone is no longer as important as it once
was in this struggle for survival itself; certainly, it is no longer
as important as social salvation. Tom, in inheriting Casy's mission and quest, comes to see that the nature of his mission is
social rather than religious (or transcendent). Perhaps Casy
had to die in order for Tom to be reborn—a familiar theme.
When Ma Joad worrisomely questions Tom as to where he
will go to seek refuge from his pursuers, Tom deemphasizes the
idea of refuge and concentrates on more vigorous and spirited

intentions. It is then that he voices his credo of the social soul, of his union (or reunion) with mankind rather than with a disembodied cosmic force:

> "I'll be all aroun' in the dark. I'll be ever'where—wherever you look. Wherever they's a fight so hungry people can eat, I'll be there. Wherever they's a cop beatin' up a guy, I'll be there. If Casy knowed, why, I'll be in the way guys yell when they're mad an'—I'll be in the way kids laugh when they're hungry an' they know supper's ready. An' when our folks eat the stuff they raise an' live in the houses they build—why, I'll be there." (p. 572)

Finally, the flood with which the novel culminates, bears within it its own symbolism; for like the flood that engulfs the Joads and other migrant families, the social soul is already beginning to absorb these scattered families, broken up, fragmented, and divided, in order to bring them together into a greater cohesive whole, prepared to engage in the struggles that lie ahead. Thus, the flight into the social soul is, in its truest sense, a flight back into a greater, more challenging reality—not for the Joads alone but for all men in their condition everywhere.

1. From THE GRAPES OF WRATH by John Steinbeck, p. 28. Copyright 1939, renewed © 1967 by John Steinbeck. Reprinted by permission of The Viking Press, Inc., and McIntosh and Otis, Inc. All further quotations are taken from this edition.

2. Hereafter, whenever I refer to the "Joad Family" or "the Joads," the terms should be taken to mean not just those members of the family bound by blood ties but also Connie Rivers, who has married into the family, and Preacher Casy who joins and identifies himself with them.

3. The biblical parallels and symbolisms of this novel have been adverted to so frequently, and with such widespread persistence on the part of so many critics, that they have virtually become common property whenever *The Grapes of Wrath* is discussed. Thus, I wish to disclaim any credit or

originality on this score and, indeed, to stress my indebtedness to all those critics whose treatments of *The Grapes of Wrath* have touched on biblical allusions and whose concerns with these have preceded mine.

4. I shall have more to say about this distinction, which is most important to the thesis that, contrary to much criticism, Tom is hardly a "transcendentalist"—in spite of those final comforting words to his mother.

chapter eight

Jake Blount:
Escape as Dead End

"But was this flight or was it onslaught?
Anyway, he was going. . . . But he would not go
too far away. He would not leave the South."

Of all the escapers discussed thus far, Jake Blount, the radical agitator in Carson McCullers's *The Heart is a Lonely Hunter* (1940), seems to be the most outlandish and the most alienated from his fellow men. In this respect he differs little from so many of the other characters in Mrs. McCullers's first novel; yet, if alienation is Jake's condition, it is a condition that not only is exemplified most obsessively in the novels and stories of Carson McCullers, but one that has been a persistent theme of many of our southern novelists. Indeed, alienation is one descriptive term that may well be applied to most escapers in the later American novel; for it seems to be in the nature of those who escape that one requirement of their condition is a restiveness, or discontent, which itself grows out of their alienation. This has certainly been characteristic of escapers like Theron Ware, George Willard, and John Andrews. But where these three were connected, no matter how tenuously, with a community of sorts—whether as in Theron Ware's congregation, George Willard's townfolk, or John Andrews's army buddies— Jake Blount is, by comparison, an escaper more in the tradition of Melville's isolato.

Jake Blount, transient and radical, is the "stranger" in this novel whose theme is alienation, for "the world of Carson McCullers is a world of outcasts. . . ." [1] But Blount is an outcast even among outcasts. Thus, what exacerbates Jake Blount's condition is the rejection he suffers at the hands of the very people he is trying to help.

Blount is not only an outcast within the town he has taken up residence in; he is a chronic wanderer, an exile, a stranger wherever he finds himself. This is apparent when we first meet him recently arrived in the town. On that occasion he asks Biff Brannon, proprietor of the New York Café, "Say, what kind of a place is this town?" [2] Although he has been in countless towns like it before, he is as ignorant of the nature of this town as if he had come from some remote land; nor will Blount ever really get to *know* the town. When he leaves it, he will depart no wiser than he was before coming to it. His question, addressed to Brannon, "Which direction is Main Street?" (p. 45), shows him to be a stranger in town on his first arrival; and although he knows the direction of Main Street when he leaves a year later, he is still a stranger. He has succeeded in communicating, or communing, with no one other than the deaf mute Singer, who, when Blount finally leaves town, is dead, a suicide.

Because of Blount's status as a stranger and a wanderer, we cannot know for sure what his origins are; indeed, it is their very vagueness that establishes him as a stranger and an outcast. Perhaps Blount himself is partly responsible for the very condition from which he is trying to free himself. When Biff Brannon asks him where he comes from, Blount's answer is a terse "Nowhere." He admits, after some badgering on Brannon's part, to being from one of the Carolinas—it is no more definite than that—but, consciously or not, he may be lying. For Blount's whole life has been a history of going from one "nowhere" to another—usually to the next town down the road.

Being a wanderer, however, Jake is homeless—not merely in the literal sense but in the sense that he seems to have little or no affiliation with a community, even the radical community where he would presumably feel more at home. Arthur Koestler, a "homeless" radical himself,[3] once applied the term to those unaffiliated radicals who, for one reason or another, doctrinal or psychological, have severed their ties to organized radical movements of the Left ("New" or old) and gone off on their own. Blount, as we shall see, certainly fits Koestler's description. On his arrival in town he leaves his suitcase for a few days with the mute Singer: this not only points up Jake's trust in this stranger—a trust others also have for Singer—but also underlines his homelessness.

Blount does not seem to have any plans for himself or a destination he can name. He does not speak of his stay in town as a temporary or permanent one, though we become progressively convinced by his actions that it will not be permanent. For Blount is a voyager without a specific port of call. We get this impression from the conversations, laconic as they are, that he has with Biff Brannon about places (real or imagined) he has been to—Texas, Oklahoma, the Carolinas, and so on. He spouts the names of towns and the places he has passed through like a drunken Walt Whitman (with whom, incongruously, he has been compared).

But this very habit of "spouting" effectively limits Blount's ability to communicate, a common failure of many of the characters in the town. Possibly one reason for Jake's alienated status—most people he comes into contact with avoid or resent him—is his self-education, biased and distorted though it is. This self-improvement places Blount beyond the pale of the mill-workers, white and black alike, many of whom are illiterate or semiliterate, the very people he would want to help. He is, as he proclaims himself to be, "a stranger in a strange land" (p. 18).

Once, Singer questions Blount on his politics by writing on a slip of paper: *"Are you Democrat or Republican?"* (p. 54). Jake's answer is to crumple the slip in his hand. The question, by Jake's standards, is meaningless, for Jake's apocalyptic politics—if "politics" it may be called—thrusts far beyond conventional party lines.

Blount is not only a homeless radical; he is a one-man organization, a leader without a following, a true "minority of one." The only person who *seems* to understand him as a person is Singer the mute; yet even Singer is hardly a supporter of

Jake's ideology. Nevertheless, the transient creates in Singer a kind of secular father confessor when he explains (or complains about) his failure to stir up enough people to follow him:

> "I been all over this place. I walk around. I talk. I try to explain to them. But what good does it do? Lord God!"
>
> He gazed into the fire, and a flush from the ale and heat deepened the color of his face. The sleepy tingling in his foot spread up his leg. He drowsed and saw the colors of the fire, the tints of green and blue and burning yellow. "You're the only one," he said dreamily. "The only one." (p. 118)

Thus, in this status—Jake Blount as one-man organization—the theme of the book is sounded; for Blount is alienated from the very people he would wish to help. The heart is indeed a lonely hunter! Blount's alienation expresses itself in the various schemes he dreams up—some of them hare-brained, such as writing chain letters—for organizing the workers for the coming revolution; sadly, though, this brand of radicalism is itself a form of alienation, cut off, as it is, from the mainstream of most radical movements of the time. His schemes are those of the crackpot. Even in his radicalism, Blount is too solipsistic for a group like the anarchists—perhaps the most alienated of radical groups in the Communist-dominated thirties; for though the anarchists were moribund at the time, they still managed to function, if only weakly, in isolated enclaves of large cities.[4] But Blount is too eccentric even for this most far-out of radical groups. The result of this isolation is that, with true monomania, Blount believes that he can overthrow the prevailing political, social, and economic system by writing chain letters to individuals who, so he hopes, will follow his example. That he never gets beyond talking about the project is some sort of indication that Blount's program for revolution appropriately fits his personality; for his talk never leads into anything more substantial than talk, or never succeeds in accomplishing the first concrete step toward a change in the social order. Indeed, it is doubtful whether a changed social order would make Blount happier, for he is an isolato who would be a stranger in any society, even one of his own making.

Dr. Mady Copeland, the Negro physician in the story, himself isolated among his own people because of his education, suspects that Blount may be demented; Copeland's suspicion does not arise from any antagonism toward Blount's philosophy —not initially, at least; indeed, there is the suggestion that, under other circumstances, he would support Blount's cause. (He has even gone so far as to name one of his own sons Karl Marx!) But Copeland's interest in Blount is the clinical interest of the physician who sees a pathological condition in the man's ravings. If Blount is not psychotic, he verges on it— so Copeland suspects. He is extreme in almost everything he does—even too extreme to make common cause with those who think as he does.

In order to avoid thinking about his own defects, Blount adopts the gospel of labor. In this respect he resembles Casy in *The Grapes of Wrath,* though in Casy's instance, the preacher is not attempting to escape anything except a former confused self. Like Casy, though, Blount had once also preached a form of evangelical Christianity. Yet if he can think in terms of society, concern himself with the mass larger than the individual, he can in effect escape from those unpalatable truths about himself. In this respect there is also some similarity between Jake Blount and the grotesques of Sherwood Anderson's Winesburg. Other than by the accident of geography and the scheme of time, Blount might have walked right out of the pages of *Winesburg;* here he reminds one of the Reverend Curtis Hartman of that work, the Godseeker who, to avoid a traumatic confrontation within his own weak soul, also expresses his religious belief in terms of the compensatory fanaticism that makes up his personality. Thus, Blount too avoids the home truth of *his* condition by embracing the "Truth" of the social condition.

Blount also is an ambiguous and ambivalent figure, for there are elements within him of the typical and the atypical escaper. In the first instance Blount is a kind of distorted Everyman, even though his claims to identity with humanity are (at least in the way he looks at that identification) preposterously self-delusive. These claims of Blount, however, are exaggerated and, one suspects, deliberately so. Given to hyperbole, Jake is a boaster and a blusterer; and if he were not so tragic a figure, one might be tempted to call him a buffoon. But his buffoonery, his use of hyperbole, his shrill boastings—these may all well be part of his "sickness," a sickness that extends far beyond the clinical complaint of solipsism, or the social complaint of alienation. Blount not only indulges in these boasts, but he does so in a spirit of hilarity. When Blount walks into Biff Brannon's New York Café accompanied by a black man, someone challenges him: "Don't you know you can't bring no nigger in a place where white men drink?" Blount's answer, characteristically, is, "I'm part nigger myself" (p. 18). Jake Blount is not interested in spearing just the bourgeoisie; his whole reason for existence seems to be predicated on shocking anyone and everyone he comes into contact with, and this, in a large measure, seems to be a possible reason for his failure to win converts and influence followers.

Unlike most of the escapers dealt with here, Jake is a habitual escaper. He is always on the move, always running. When we first meet him, he has just arrived in the nameless town (modeled, allegedly, on Carson McCullers's hometown of Columbus, Georgia), presumably after a flight from a town he has just left behind; and when the book ends, he is on his way out of town, this time his flight possessing a more serious reason (he may have killed a man). He has first fled home as a ten-year-old; as a full-grown man, he is still on the move—full-grown physically, but emotionally still very much the ten-year-old who left home years earlier.

Unlike other escapes—say, Huck's, George Willard's, or at a further remove, Theron Ware's—those of Blount do not seem to bring about in him any spiritual regeneration; he seems to remain what he was before the escapes—even to the extent of suffering from the same delusions (or illusions) he had suffered from before his final escape becomes necessary. When he leaves town at the end of the book, he still thinks of organizing the masses in a great crusade to overthrow capitalism; he seems to have learned nothing from his experiences in the town. Again, unlike those of other escapers, Jake's escapes are neither resurrective nor initiatory: they are the chronic condition of his life.

Like so many escapers, Blount is isolated by his own peculiarities and eccentricities as much as by those who react to those eccentricities. However, there is the paradox that when Jake does have the opportunity to escape, or leave town under somewhat more auspicious circumstances than those of his final departure, he doesn't grasp the opportunity. When spring comes, Blount, purely in terms of fantasy, feels that it would be a good time to go out West—one traditional egress for the American escaper—or south to the Gulf of Mexico. But he does neither. It is almost as if he were suffering from a kind of paralysis that keeps him in the town until something drastic enough should come along to free him from that paralysis.

Jake Blount is also a walker and a talker, although it is the first of these traits that seems to be more typical of most escapers. As with them, walking and talking for Jake become ways of escaping an untenable self. His compulsive need to walk the streets of the town is brought about by his restlessness, his inability to stay put or to settle down. It is a common complaint so many escapers seem to suffer from; we have seen it in such diverse characters as John Andrews, Theron Ware, and George Willard. For example, when the room Blount sleeps in becomes, in its lonely isolation, too much of a burden for him—that is, when it becomes *too* peaceful, *too* comfortable— he must get out to walk by himself for a while. When the five o'clock whistles blow and workers are on their way home for the night, Jake "usually . . . [does] not stay at home . . . [but goes] out into the narrow, empty streets" (p. 119).

But if Jake is a walker, he is certainly more active, if not very effective, as a talker. As a talker, Jake has the philosophy of the itinerant radical, a type long familiar on the American scene, whose roots go back not only to the Wobblies and the Knights of Labor but to those who, with something of the same intensity of fire and zeal—the gospel revivalists—campaigned up and down the land in an earlier century. Indeed, as previously suggested, before Jake had discovered the gospel of labor, he had persuaded himself that he wanted to preach the gospel of Christ. However, when he discovers the principles of the radical labor movement "It was like being born a second time" (p. 117). In spite of the secularization of Jake's concerns for the welfare of humanity, the religious overtones are constantly present, even in Jake's talk:

> "The things they have done to us! [he tells Singer]. The truths they have turned into lies. The ideals they have fouled and made vile. Take Jesus. He was one of us. He knew. When he said that it is harder for a camel to pass through the eye of a needle than for a rich man to enter the kingdom of God—he damned well meant just what he said.[5] But look what the Church has done to Jesus during the last two thousand years. What they have made of him. How they have turned every word he spoke for their own vile ends. Jesus would be framed and in jail if he

was living today. Jesus would be one who really knows. Me and Jesus would sit across the table and I would look at him and he would look at me and we would both know that the other knew. Me and Jesus and Karl Marx could all sit at a table. . . ." (p. 122)

The further irony of Blount's status as a talker is that he is unable (or empirically appears unable) to communicate his gospel of labor to those whom it would most seem to benefit— the laborers themselves. Yet one difficulty that Blount seems to have is his status as a "performer," an exhibitionist, yelling in the street at the top of his lungs, challenging everyone he comes into contact with to find a false note in his message. Unlike the King and the Duke in *Huckleberry Finn,* Jake Blount does not have the power to attract people to his pitch. Either people have become less naïve, or Jake is simply ineffectual; there is the suspicion, however, that it is Blount's ineffectiveness that is more to blame than any lack of perception on the part of his audience. But if Blount is unlike the King and the Duke in his greater sincerity, he too, like them, is eventually forced to leave town, in flight from what he believes to be a pursuing law.

Further, Jake's status as a talker shows us a man who seems to possess the "gift of tongues";[6] but unlike preacher Casy in *The Grapes of Wrath,* there seems to be no one around for him to preach to, or whom he can reach when he does try to preach—unless it be Singer, who, in any event, is not particularly interested in Jake's message. Since no one of any consequence to Jake's cause seems willing to listen to him, he must finally talk to himself, or break out into those wild shouting marathons so characteristic of his periodic drunken binges.

This walled-in feeling, of being cut off from the world, produces in Jake a feeling of desperation, which finally bursts forth in belligerence. For Blount is the Unrequited Lover, a frustrated quester, even, as has been suggested, a "tragic savior." Perhaps he fits into all three categories, especially since his love for the working class is rejected by that class; like so many rejected suitors, Blount suffers from the frenzies of these rejections and slights to his vanity. He would, of course, like to be loved, or at lease admired, by the exploited workers. But they fail to accommodate Jake; indeed, on one occasion, they even turn their full fury upon him.

Blount is certainly a would-be savior of sorts, but a savior without a people to save, for he has been rejected (by the people) in that role. He is, however, as much a Christ figure— in his own perverse way—as is Singer (who is generally thought to fulfiill that role). Apart from the symbol of his "stigmata," caused by an act of violent self-destruction years earlier, Jake's message is that "the truth shall make you free"— Jake's brand of truth, that is. Like Jesus, though certainly not for the same reasons, Jake is rejected and "despised of men"; he is cast out by the people whom he would save—in a sense "crucified" by them. Jake certainly echoes the Christ when he tells Copeland, if not very originally, "It's this way. This is how I see it. The only solution is for the people to *know*. Once they know the truth they can be oppressed no longer. Once just half of them know the whole fight is won" (p. 229).

Although Jake shares with the other characters in the book the sense of alienation and isolation, and the need for love that grows out of that condition, what is most characteristic of him, and least characteristic of the others, is his condition of chronic itinerancy, his constant need to light out, to escape his previous place and condition. Although each of the characters in this book of loneliness is searching for something, none is an escaper in quite the formal sense as is Jake.[7] For Blount's first escape is, at one level, quite literal and real: it is a physical escape; indeed, a flight from the forces—specifically the law—that seem to threaten him in the town. At another level, however, it is also an escape from the hopelessness that the town represents for him. As an afterthought one might add that of the eight escapers dealt with in this study, six, including Jake, attempt in one way or another an escape from the law as part of their larger escapes. These are, of course, Huck (even if he is not an official fugitive from justice); Frederick Henry (from the Italian military police); John Andrews (from the American military police); Tom Joad (from both Arkansas and California lawmen); and Bigger Thomas—discussed in chapter 9—(from a Chicago police dragnet).

One of the individuals with whom Blount may be able to make some contact is Dr. Benedict Mady Copeland, the Negro physician. Yet in almost every instance in which Blount attempts to make such a contact, his effort is doomed to failure. Both Jake and Copeland even go so far—begrudgingly enough—as to get together over the common need to organize blacks and whites. But even here, Copeland's blackness and Jake's whiteness prove a barrier; Copeland distrusts Blount the white man, whom he has come to think of as synonymous with oppression; and Blount in his blindness would ignore the ethnic problem as needing a special approach as distinct from that of the larger, more generalized political and economic struggle. To Blount, Copeland as a Negro is—to borrow Ralph Ellison's term—an "invisible man." Since color, in Blount's eyes, has little or no substantial reality or relevance in the class struggle (that is, the exploited black man is the brother of the exploited white man; therefore, why should one stress the very thing that separates them?), he refuses to see it as having any reality or pertinence in the greater struggle for freedom. Blount sees the struggle purely in terms of class; Copeland, in terms of race.

One person with whom Blount seems to have established some sort of relationship is Singer, the mute. Once Singer removes himself from the scene—his suicide toward the end of the novel—the world flies apart for Jake, who, in spite of his social concerns, is ultimately conquered by the understanding (or *apparent* understanding) and love of an individual. It is only after Singer's death that Jake's real troubles commence, for the mute's death releases a wildness in Blount that causes him to steer straight for his own disaster, as though he were trying to compensate for the loss of Singer. As he does for most of the characters, Singer represents for Blount all of the understanding and compassion that Jake cannot find in others. It is of no consequence that Singer may not be any of these things; it is enough that Blount feels that he is.

Relations between Jake and some of the other characters are less ambiguous. Though we do not for a certainty know Singer's opinion of Blount, except that he has the sort of pity for him that one would have for a helpless child, we do get a more substantial notion of Biff Brannon's opinion of him. When Alice Brannon, Biff's wife, accuses Blount of being a bum and a freak, Brannon's rejoinder is, "I like freaks" (p. 12). But, thinks Brannon, a little further on:

> Blount was not a freak, although when you first saw him he gave you that impression. It was like something was deformed about him—but when you looked at him closely each part of him was normal and as it ought to be. Therefore if this difference was not in the body it was probably in the mind. He was like a man who had served a term in prison or had been to Harvard College or had lived for a long time with foreigners in South America. He was like a person who had been somewhere that other people are not likely to go or had done something that others are not apt to do. (pp. 16–17)

In Brannon there seems to be not only a compassion, which Singer seems to embody, but an understanding—blurred as it is—that we are never sure Singer has, in spite of his much-vaunted sense of "penetration" into the town's characters.

The drunken brawl, which turns into a race riot at the carnival grounds where Jake works as the operator of a flying jinny, leads directly to Blount's escape from the town. Although there are probably more subtle reasons for Jake's flight, it is the riot that finally acts as the immediate trigger mechanism of that flight. The battle that Blount gets himself into doesn't even involve a principle. In its drunken precipitousness it reminds one of the brawl that Tom Joad got himself into, in which he kills a man. But in Tom's second involvement—his killing of a California deputy sheriff—he strikes out as much from principle as from anger.[8] Blount's involvement in the riot is a blind striking-out, having no more principle than Blount himself has when he is wallowing in his drunken bouts. He flails out blindly and wildly at anyone, black or white, who happens to be within easy reach of his fists. And the riot itself, in its purposelessness and insane idiocy, seems to symbolize within Blount the degeneration of his purpose: at the risk of producing what is most likely a bad alliterative pun, Blount's purpose has been "blunted," perhaps by the very bluntness that seems to be characteristic both of his inspiration and his misfortune. At this point his revolutionary aims—if they were ever clear-cut to begin with—have degenerated into a free-for-all. There is now, if indeed there ever has been, no order to his revolt against the meaning of the social order, which, according to Blount, lacks all order. And when he sees close by on the fairgrounds a dead Negro boy, Blount, perhaps as a result of the general confusion, panics. Realizing all too clearly the possibilities of a frame-up—especially since his handwritten handbills carrying his revolutionary message are scattered about the fairgrounds—Jake makes his escape from the town.

The arrival of the police at the fairgrounds acts as an immediate spur to his decision to run away—blindly, hysterically, down the dark twisted streets of the town. He has no destination, no plans, his flight being a stark, panic-stricken run to get out of the immediate area. And so when he finally determines to escape the town itself, that decision is made precipitously—as it has been in most of the escapes—on the spur of the moment, on impulse. There is little, if any, conscious planning involved. When he finally does leave, Blount doesn't have the slightest notion of where he is bound.

There is another ingredient in Jake's escape: his false hope. Apparently he has not learned anything significant from his experience, either in terms of survival or enlightened self-interest. Even at the moment of his departure, he still carries the hope—to be sure, somewhat battered by now—that he will eventually succeed in his effort to get the people to rise up against the venal social order; thus the hope is both self-consolation for his previous failures and nourishment for Jake's self-delusion. Yet as hopeless as that hope is, Blount is both the master and the slave of the vision that drives him on and that eventually will lead to a dead end—for himself if not for his dream.

With the blindness of the fanatic who will not learn from his previous experience, and with the same infinite ability to rationalize, Blount tenaciously hangs onto his apparently unshakable faith. In this respect it is a grotesque parody of the faith of previous generations in the future of America. For in spite of his optimism—and he is still an optimist when we last view him making his exit from the town—that optimism is an ironic commentary on Blount's condition, since optimism in this period of national crisis is no longer a viable position nor a salable product.

Thus, when Jake leaves town, his faith in the future is an illusory one, and it will probably serve him as falsely as it has thus far served him. Naturally, that obsessive—monomaniacal?

—hope is projected upon the town that lies up (or down) the road where, again, so he desperately trusts, the people will hopefully give him the hearing they have thus far denied him in all of the towns he has left behind. Blount, however, fails to see that all the towns are alike, for they inevitably project back at him the image he constructs of them. That his contempt (for the people in those towns) is an ingredient of that image can plainly be seen in his experiences in the town he has lived in for the past year. In this respect Theron Ware, in *his* year's stay in Octavius, also sees the small town in terms of mutual rejection; but where Theron has some substantial notion of where he is bound, Jake hasn't. In this, of course, what once held an ingredient of hope now shows us despair, even though it is disguised as the slenderest of hope.

Further, the scene of his departure is not one that would under ordinary circumstances encourage such optimism, for it takes place against a backdrop of poverty and desolation—a southern wasteland:

> He walked until he reached the railroad tracks. On either side there were rows of dilapidated two-room houses. In the cramped back yards were rotted privies and lines of torn, smoky rags hung out to dry. For two miles there was not one sight of comfort or space or cleanliness. Even the earth itself seemed filthy and abandoned. Now and then there were signs that a vegetable row had been attempted, but only a few withered collards had survived. And a few fruitless, smutty fig trees. Little younguns swarmed in this filth, the smaller of them stark naked. The sight of this poverty was so cruel and hopeless that Jake snarled and clenched his fists. (p. 266)

Why things should be any different in the next town only Jake could possibly know. But it seems to solace him that the poverty that taunts his failure in this town will only inspire him further in the next. Hope—attenuated though it is—remains where faith has fled.

Unlike those of so many escapers, Jake's escape seems to be a rather tame and unimaginative one; for unlike those escapers who have gone before, Jake no longer has the urge to move completely out of the immediate geographical region he has always presumably lived in, the South. Unlike Theron Ware who, at the end of his stay in Octavius, is Seattle bound, Jake doesn't really seem to wish for a new start that a complete change of scene might make possible. Instead, his escape seems feeble compared with those previous escapes we have examined, an escape essentially turned in on itself. It has led into a dead end geographically, physically, and spiritually:

> But where would it be this time? The names of cities called to him—Memphis, Wilmington, Gastonia, New Orleans. He would go somewhere. *But not out of the South.* . . . It was different this time. *He did not long for open space and freedom—just the reverse.* (p. 261; italics added)

Like so many escapers, Blount is an embodiment of the aspirations of the American dream; but now the aspirations, if not the dream, have gone sour. Jake Blount is, and has been for a long time, a self-appointed "circuit rider" of the class struggle; in another time he might literally have been a circuit rider, a preacher of religious revivalism, which had indeed almost been his destiny. But now he is a Jim Casy without that individual's gift for attracting followers. What is even more ironic (and bitter) for Jake is that he proves to be a failure at the very kind of preaching—of the revolutionary Word—in a time when that Word possessed a great potential audience, in the days of the Great Depression. Yet even under these "felicitous" circumstances, Jake Blount is a failure.

Blount's job as a flying-jinny operator in a carnival outwardly seems to reveal and symbolize his inner condition, for neither as preacher nor as dreamer has Jake been particularly successful. Even his job seems to parody the original bright dream, to be seen in the details of that job. He must run the machinery that rotates wooden horses; but as part of that job he must keep the crowds from getting out of hand. Yet he proves a failure even in this. Further, the job lacks color or a sense of adventure. As such, it becomes a grotesque parody of the earlier promise of the American dream whose horses saw vaster visions than those circumscribed by the limits of a fairground. Jake's horses are gimcrack and wooden—steeds for children, drunks, and tired mill-hands to ride on.

Thus, the end of the American dream for Jake Blount also leads to his own dead end. In Steinbeck's *The Grapes of Wrath* the Joads at least have some small initial hope. But in spite of his implied affirmation of hope on leaving town—"There was hope in him"—Jake Blount is truly in a hopeless predicament. Whatever hope is left in him is ultimately a mocking echo of a lost dream, designed to instill in him the necessary fortitude for what lies ahead. When Huck Finn, George Willard, or even the flaccid Theron Ware light out, the escape takes the form of an aspiration—to reach a territory, to go to a big city, to head west to sell real estate or go into politics. This cannot be said of Jake Blount. He is forced out of the town before he can construct a plan or a program for himself for the destination that lies farther than down the road. Thus, for Jake the American dream has truly faded, and all he can ever do, or be capable of doing, is to rant against the status quo that the dream has become.

Blount's defeat may therefore be seen as the defeat of a greater dream that once gave America and Americans the necessary hope and courage to rediscover new values in the discovery (or rediscovery) of a new land. If the defeat is not to be permanent, then a new life and a reason for living must be infused into those escapers who are to come, who will attempt not only to escape their own untenable predicaments, but to aid their fellow Americans to do so: if there is to be, as Sinclair

Lewis once put it, "a passionate escape there must be not only a place from which to flee but a place to which to flee." Today, in America, the escape has become more than simply a geographic quest; it has become a spiritual one—and not alone for the individual but for the nation. Thus, escape, if it is to lead to the rebirth of a greater hope, must not only be away from something, but a thrust toward something incomparably better than the landscape of the past or the shores of the present.

1. Catharine Hughes, "A World of Outcasts," *Commonweal*, 13 October 1961, p. 73.

2. Carson McCullers, *The Heart is a Lonely Hunter* (Boston, 1940), p. 17. Used with the permission of the Houghton Mifflin Company. All further quotations are taken from this edition.

3. *The Yogi and the Commissar* (New York, 1945), p. 97, Collier Book Edition.

4. The anarchists of pre–World War II years were totally unlike the current crop of Weatherman *enragés,* tending more toward the heated cafeteria table talk than to the kind of mindless violence of recent years. Indeed, many prewar anarchists were actually gentle, dreamy souls.

5. As an instance of Blount's half-digested knowledge, his quotation, or paraphrase, is slightly, but critically, off-center: what Jesus is really supposed to have said is that it is *easier* for a camel to go through the eye of a needle than for a rich man to enter the kingdom of God.

6. It is a perverse "gift" in Blount's case, since it drives people away from him instead of drawing them to him.

7. Harry Minowitz, Mick Kelly's young seducer, may be thought of as an escaper too. But his is an escape through panic—ill-founded—that he may have made Mick pregnant; besides, his role in the story is a minor one, hardly large enough to justify any expanded treatment here.

8. Significantly, when Tom does strike, he does so as a man of few words. In spite of his key role in *The Grapes of Wrath,* he is a terse, laconic individual; Jake, on the other hand, though he talks a lot, never seems to accomplish much, even in the negative way of a Tom Joad.

chapter nine

Bigger Thomas:
Escape into the Labyrinth

"Sometimes, in his own room or on the sidewalk,
the world seemed to him a strange labyrinth. . . ."

The condition of the black man in America in the last three hundred years has been one of perennial escape, either geographically, as in Jim's escape in *Huckleberry Finn,* or spiritually, through the church or away from the law. Only in recent years has the black American chosen to confront his (and white America's) problems head-on, no matter how painful the encounter. In Richard Wright's *Native Son* (1940), we are shown the life of the black man in microcosm, when that life had begun to converge on a point that brought two irreconcilables together: abject docility and explosive rebellion. As for the latter—to paraphrase a slogan of a generation ago, it is better to die fighting on your feet than to live a slave on your knees—the implied slogan of today's black liberation movement makes an even more specific appeal: it is better to stand and fight for your human rights than to escape into the old condition—even at the cost of life itself.

Heretofore, all of the escapes we have discussed have been from country to city, from village to town, and from rivers to Alpine countries and territories ahead. But for Bigger Thomas, the protagonist of Wright's *Native Son,* escape takes place *within* the urban labyrinth that has come to be called the black ghetto. In effect, his escape has been blocked; it is doomed to failure even before it begins. In this sense *Native Son* is one of the few purely naturalistic novels that contains within it a strong escape motif. There are others—the novels of Dreiser, Norris, and Crane; but in them the escape is an ancillary rather than a major motif.

Yet *Native Son* is only superficially an escape novel in the usual sense—a novel in which the hero sets out on a geographical journey or quest in order to leave behind an untenable situation for one that promises improvement. At a deeper level, Bigger Thomas's escape—what there is of it—is an escape into the subterranean side of his own nature, an exploration into his own inner "heart of darkness," which has brought on the implosion of rage, and which finally explodes in an act of violence perpetrated on a world that Bigger has justifiably come to hate.

The opening scene of the novel is set in an urban tenement— a setting that could hardly be more appropriate for an act of escape—as distinct from those bucolic and semibucolic landscapes where most of the escapes dealt with in this study have taken place. This is the scene where the rat—that repulsive symbol of daily (and nightly!) life in the black ghetto— appears. The rat itself almost arouses our *sympathy,* as Bigger, who attempts to trap and kill him, will later arouse a similar compassion. However, the rat, as despicable as he is, is still a living thing. As such, if he merits revulsion, he also merits compassion; for not unexpectedly, both Bigger and the rat are (in the naturalistic mode) "victims of circumstance," inheritors of a "world they never made," blind creatures, threshing against an inscrutable force that would destroy them both, a world they would happily escape from given the opportunity. Of course, the rat of Book I will become Bigger himself. For like that rat, he too is trapped, in the first and in the last instance. Trapped as he is, however, he will try to escape his predetermined fate; and like the rat, he too will be destroyed by a frightened, uncomprehending (white) world.

What are some of the impelling and compelling forces that drive Bigger into choosing the futile path of this form of escape? For one thing—implicitly and later explicitly—Bigger is in revolt, not only against the white world but against his family—his younger brother, his sister, and his religious mother, the last of whom represents the escapism of resignation to her centuries-old condition of chattel and psychological slavery. All embody for Bigger the sordid tenement life he dreams of escaping. The dream, however, remains well within the province of dream, since at this time in his country and the country's social development, a more viable, constructive escape for a black man was out of the question.

One occupational hazard of urban life is boredom. "Nothing ever happens," Bigger complains early in the book.[1] And it is partly the escape from boredom that Bigger not only wants but needs; yet the movies he goes to from time to time in order to escape that boredom—they are fantasies in themselves, representing, as they do, the lives of an idle white elite rather than the lives of most white people—only act as temporary, ultimately unsatisfactory anodynes. For movies are a poor substitute for a more concrete, happier reality; silver screen projections are no more realizable in life than are Theron Ware's yacht-filled fantasies.

The impulses toward violence within Bigger are already apparent in Book I ("Fear"). At first we see the manifestation of those impulses in the pleasure he takes in killing the rat—certainly one of a number of displacements of his hostility toward the larger world. Here, unlike his status in that world, he is master of the situation; he it is who arrogates to himself the power of a god to deal out death. Then there is the attack on a member of his own gang, Gus, in which Bigger manipulates Gus as a ventriloquist would a rag doll. In these two scenes we are aware of Bigger's rage bubbling to the surface in what might have been considered (in the ghetto of the 1930s) a calculated though "acceptable" minor explosion for the white society to absorb. After all, he assaults "only" another black man—all too reminiscent of Huck's reply when asked by Aunt Sally if anyone had been hurt by the boiler explosion aboard a river steamboat: "No'm. Killed a nigger." In each case the rage and the violence that stem from it are unrestrained. But even these are insufficient to provide a complete release for Bigger's surge toward freedom. Unhappily for Bigger—and others—that freedom can only be found in the killing of a white woman. Bigger is not so naïve as to think he has the ghost of a chance of escaping the inevitable guilty death-penalty verdict of an all-white jury if he is tried and caught. Yet when the time comes to face that alternative, he is willing to accept the consequences of his act—as "willing" that is, as one can be under such circumstances. Bigger, of course, wants no more to die than does anyone else; but he has been placed in a position where he would rather die than continue the death-farce that is called his "life." He is Camus's stranger, though without the degree of self-knowledge that Meursault is eventually granted for a fleeting moment before *his* end.

Bigger's escape is not just from the scene of his crime. When the time comes for his flight, a realization dawns: "It was familiar, this running away. All his life he had been knowing that sooner or later something like this would come to him. And now, here it was. He had always felt outside of this white world, and now it was true. It made things simple" (pp. 187–88).

As for Bigger's mother's escapism into religious fundamentalism, even before the novel opens, Bigger has already rejected it. Like Huck Finn, who also felt "there ain't nothing to it," Bigger is too involved in the realities of the present to embrace either his mother's brand of religion or that other, secular, messianic "by-and-by," Jan Erlone's communism—the very catalyst that brought the seeds of Bigger's fruitless rebellion to life.[2]

Bigger's girl Bessie is somewhat more realistic in terms of their short-range goals; she recognizes that their blackness makes it virtually impossible for them to escape either the ghetto or their condition. However, as part of his escape fantasy, Bigger resorts to the possibility of extorting ransom money—ten thousand dollars—from the parents of the dead

Mary Dalton. But even if Bigger manages to pull off the ransom plan—extremely unlikely under the circumstances—his escape would only be an escape from one ghetto into another. In contrast, the high point of Bigger's substantive escape (as distinct from his fantasies) is his mental and metaphysical condition, which parallels that of John Andrews in Dos Passos's *Three Soldiers*. Like Andrews in the earlier novel—there may have been some influence on Wright here—Bigger never feels so free as he does in the hours just prior to his capture, even though he knows the inevitability and imminence of his end.

Bigger's early fantasies, then, may correctly be called fantasies of escapism, as distinguished from true escape; the former are almost purely composed of daydreams with no resultant action, whereas the latter, as we have suggested elsewhere, leads to an action, even if it has been preceded by *well-thought-out* "daydreams" (abstract, rather than concrete, plans). One of these fantasies—over which Bigger and his pool-hall companions have some fun—lies in Bigger's imitation of whites in strategic positions of power most whites do not enjoy. Among these are the president of the United States; an army general; J. P. Morgan playing the stocks or, more likely, manipulating and buying them. All of these in a sense are Shrike-like suggestions (as in the false opportunities for escape set forth by the character Shrike in Nathanael West's *Miss Lonelyhearts*). Bigger, however, has the satisfaction of play-acting, of "having fun," or *poking* fun at the white world that has cheated the black man out of his share of these perquisites. This is one way—a relatively harmless way—of getting back at the world without being taken to task for those antics by that world.

Bigger's fantasies of "escape" take a number of other forms: one of these lies in the pool hall and the gang he hangs out with there; another lies, as already suggested, in the movies he goes to see rather regularly: "In a movie he could dream without effort; all he had to do was lean back in a seat and keep his eyes open" (p. 12). That is, the darkened theater becomes an opiate of forgetfulness for Bigger, a comfortable womb where he can enjoy a state of near oblivion. A third lies in his dreams of making money through petty burglary and, ultimately, armed robbery. One of these fantasies concerns something that Bigger knows he will never have the opportunity to try: fly an airplane that skywrites, like the one he sees doing that job in the early part of the novel. The sky-writing plane becomes for him a symbol of the unattainable freedom he craves but will never enjoy. Given the plight of the overwhelmingly vast majority of black people in the 1930s—and for that matter, many whites in that time of widespread economic distress—it is highly doubtful that Bigger will ever seriously be able to entertain that ambition. Thus, Bigger can never make this kind of escape a consequential act, except in the fantasy of escapism. And when he does make his lunge into flight, we know that his flight (from his pursuers and the law) and escape are not necessarily synonymous in Bigger's case; that unlike such flights (from the law) as Tom Joad's, Bigger's is hopeless. For when Joad escapes, it is from one reality into another, no matter how hard or undesirable that second reality is. Tom, in that final escape of his, has a sense of mission—to lift up his people. Bigger's "escapes" (before they turn into concrete flight) are largely from harsh fact into euphoric fantasy. One reason that Bigger's escape can never be as effective as Joad's is our knowledge that

> Bigger cannot "escape," as Tom Joad can, for he cannot find the community which the Joads discover on the road. The only community he faces is a machine-like mob, white and black.[3]

Bigger's attempt to escape his trap comes up against a wall of frustration that separates him from wider opportunities and the possibility of a way out: "But what could he do? Each time he asked himself that question his mind hit a blank wall and he stopped thinking" (p. 11). The way out is constantly blocked: to be a flyer one must be white. To do *anything* outside the role his society has assigned to him, he has to be white.

Another symbol of freedom, as unattainable as flying an airplane, is the pigeon Bigger watches early in the novel, which, like the airplane, can also fly. Free as a bird is no idle phrase for Bigger, for this bird, like the plane, represents another kind of freedom to Bigger, notwithstanding the fact that both bird and plane are themselves subject to the laws of gravity and aerodynamics. Of course, Bigger's sense of the symbolic, if it is not subtle, is certainly not designed to place any restrictions (physical or spiritual) on what he *feels* to be the freedom others enjoy.

Although Bigger is not overly enthusiastic at being hired as a chauffeur by the Dalton family, he takes the job, for the relief agency has confronted him with the certainty of having his family cut off relief if he refuses. However, as coercive as it is, this may be a kind of provisional escape from the ghetto—a room of his own in the huge house of a wealthy white family. Yet that escape is always provisional, never complete. The white world—the Dalton house, the luxury of that house, its neighborhood—is an incomprehensible and threatening world to Bigger; it makes him feel vulnerable and exposed, even though the Dalton's are supposed to be in favor of improving the lot of the black man. In short, the ghetto is ambiguously both trap and womb, offering imprisonment and superficial security.

Bigger's act of murder is *itself* the climax of Bigger's true escape, even though, paradoxically, it is the initial step of his escape too. In the works discussed previously, the climax takes place with the decision to escape and the escaper acting on that decision. In Bigger's case the climax to the escape comes *before* any concrete plan for escape has been worked out, or even before the actual escape itself. The climax of the escape actually lies in the murder of the Dalton girl, even before Bigger flees—indeed, the actual flight itself is muted, presented in low key, played down. True, a paradox of sorts. Yet unlike the flight that follows the act of violence and the built-in fantasies that are born in Bigger as a result of the flight, the killing of Mary Dalton, a white woman, is itself a psychologically liberating act for Bigger:

> His act of murder seems to him to have released immense potentialities that had lain imprisoned within his personality. While he is actually running away from pursuit in desperation, he conceives himself to be a Tamburlaine capable of reducing the whole world to the prostrate state it had imposed upon him and he has now escaped. He seems now to be flying the forbidden airplane above a remote and impotent world.[4]

In short, the act of murder itself has become the liberative trigger mechanism of his escape, and thus a climax to it too.

After Mary Dalton's murder, Bigger talks to Bessie about the possibility of leaving town with the hoped-for ransom money. He offers to split the swag with her if she will help him in his bid for freedom. However, assuming that they manage to make good on their (actually Bigger's) ransom plans, and are relatively successful in fleeing the immediate locality, Bigger's escape, ultimately, can only be an escape to the edge of the ghetto, not beyond it. In the ghetto there is a sort of security (weak as that security is)in relative anonymity; beyond the pale of the ghetto, he would be exposed to an even greater vulnerability than he is within the ghetto—as Yakov Bok, in Bernard Malamud's *The Fixer,* discovers under similar circumstances but, of course, for other reasons. Yet his escape, even within the ghetto, can only be, like the

ghetto itself, labyrinthine. It will turn out to be nothing more
than an escape from one dead end to another, inasmuch as
another ghetto would not be much more secure than his present
one.

The real escape of Bigger finally lies in his existential act of
double murder. If Mary Dalton's murder was an ambiguous
act, almost accidental in its lack of planning, cold intention,
and execution, then the murder of Bessie comes within the
wider province of cold choice—that is, the rationalization is
present in Bigger that Bessie will be a drag on any effort he
might make to get far enough away; that, in fact, she would
be more hindrance than help. Thus, he must get rid of her before
she can talk. This is the critical act that reinforces Bigger's
existential sense of freedom. Like Camus's rebel, he too acts
to counter society's "no" with his own. Thus:

> Out of it all, over and above all that had happened, impalpable
> but real, there remained to him a queer sense of power. *He* had
> done this. *He* had brought all this about. In all of his life these
> two murders were the most meaningful things that had ever hap-
> pened to him. He was living, truly and deeply. . . . (p. 203)

Yet this escape through violence is self-defeating—obviously!
As Robert Bone puts it, it is "an escape that never really gets
beyond the perimeters of the Black ghetto." [5] Yet Bigger's
rebellion may be traced back immediately to the discrepancy
between Bigger's half-believed-in dreams and the reality his
society offers him. As Albert Camus sees it, "The spirit of
rebellion can exist only in a society where a theoretical equality
conceals great factual inequalities." [6] Concludes Camus: "With
rebellion, awareness [i.e., sight] is born." [7]

To turn to the visual metaphor, often noted in the critical
literature on *Native Son,* the others in this tragedy of multi-
dimensional blindness are blind too—either literally, as in

Mrs. Dalton's case, or figuratively, as in the instances of Mary Dalton, Jan Erlone her friend, and even the more socially aware Communist defense lawyer, Max. All "see" Bigger through their own astigmatic vision of life, which in the crisis proves to be totally inadequate for an analysis of Bigger's rage and the hang-ups that make for it. Even Max, who perhaps comes closer than the others to something of an answer to Bigger's enigma—his Marxist view of the part that social and economic determinism plays—does not even touch the ancillary but equally important psychopathological problems that impel Bigger to become the thing that society has made of him and that sooner or later society must confront if it hopes to save not just its Biggers but itself. The liberation that Bigger experiences by his "rebellion" (i.e., the murder of two women) is not quite the expression of revolutionary insurgence—at least in terms of Old Left theory as distinct from New Left practice —that even Max the (Old Left) Communist lawyer had bargained for; liberation, in the parlance of the time, should primarily liberate the "masses," not the self. In the logic of the revolutionary ethos (of the thirties), by participating in the liberation of the masses, one ultimately liberates *oneself*. Again, in dealing with the rebellion of the individual, which hardly cleaves to any party line, Camus puts it this way: "Rebellion . . . breaks the seal and allows the whole being to come into play. It liberates stagnant waters and turns them into a raging torrent." [8] Thus, Bigger's rebellion not only liberates him psychologically but gives him a sense of possibility—dubious though that sense is—that nothing else can. Further, Bigger resembles Camus's rebel far more than he does Frantz Fanon's *conscious* (or class-conscious) colonial rebel. For "up to this point he [the rebel] has at least remained silent and has abandoned himself to the form of despair in which a condition is accepted even though it is considered unjust." [9] The rebel is not rebelling against what James Baldwin has called a "previous condition"; he is attempting to *escape* it. Bigger's escape (or rebellion)—the two are used interchangeably here—may be thought of as coming within the metaphysically existential province of choice, although Wright, at the time he wrote the book, probably did not consciously or deliberately conceive of Bigger in those terms. Certainly, Bigger himself does not think of escape, consciously or otherwise, in those terms.

After Bigger takes the plunge into violence, Chicago's South Side becomes for him a labyrinth—Wright's word—from which there is no egress. Almost before he makes his first bid for freedom, he knows, more instinctively than rationally, that there is no true or lasting escape for him. Like the rat in the book's first pages, Bigger is trapped—except that he is no rat but a human being caught in the grip of circumstances in a world he might have shared were life ordered in some other, more equitable way:

> He could not leave Chigago; all roads were blocked, and all trains, buses and autos were being stopped and searched.
>
> .   .   .   .
>
> He was trapped. He would have to get out of this building. But where would he go? (p. 208)

Trapped. There is an irony here, since even the more familiar and innocuous amusement park labyrinth (or maze) has a way out, as well as a way in, assuming that one does not panic and disorient himself in the process of finding it. In Bigger's instance, the "escape" itself finally ends by becoming Bigger's greatest trap. Indeed—and it is doubtful how consciously aware Bigger is of this—if he would escape from the labyrinth of the city and society, he must first escape from the labyrinth of his own mind. But when he "blows his mind," as the saying has it, he has temporarily found an escape of sorts. However, even that

escape demands murder rather than creation; an act of desperation rather than an act of imagination. Mary Dalton may have
been a crude do-gooder, a guilt-ridden liberal-turned-fellow-
traveler and later Communist, even a stupidly blind representative of the exploitative society. But apart from her naïveté
and her innocence, she is not so evil or so hypocritical that she
deserves to suffer violent death for that lack at the hands of a
victim, even though in her bumbling, good-intentioned (but
blind) way, she was trying to help that victim.

The buildings in the black ghetto where Bigger hopes to hide
out are more than just a symbolic labyrinth from which he
comes, and from which he hopes to escape: "There were many
empty buildings with black windows, like *blind eyes*, buildings
like skeletons standing with snow on their bones in the winter
winds" (pp. 147–48; italics added). But Wright moves beyond the image of the labyrinth to the city as jungle. In the
scene where Bessie desperately tries to get him to decide on
where they should hide, Bigger suggests they occupy one of the
condemned tenement houses. "There's plenty of 'em," he tells
her. "It'll be like hiding in a jungle" (p. 193). Thus, the urban
escape turns into an escape from the twentieth century itself.
The escape here has mythic overtones—an escape into a Congo
of the soul, a kind of Emperor Jones fantasy of man attempting
to escape the very fate he has already set in motion. Yet the
abiding and overarching image is that of escape into a city
that is already "like . . . a jungle"—or a labyrinth.

After his discovery, Bigger jumps from rooftop to rooftop
in his attempt to evade his pursuers, dodging behind chimneys
—all part of the experience of a man caught in a labyrinth. For
the urban labyrinth is only an extension of the ghetto labyrinth,
the ghetto itself a microcosm of the larger labyrinthine world
of the city. "History has many cunning passages, contrived
corridors," says T. S. Eliot in "Gerontion," and Bigger finds

this to be true of the city and the ghetto that are at once his life and symbolic of it. That is, like history's "cunning passages"—something also created by men—so the labyrinth contains within it the cruelly deceptive suggestion of hope for a way out.

Blindness itself is a labyrinth, or symbol of it. We might start with Mrs. Dalton's literal (and symbolic) blindness, which precipitates Bigger's first panicky act and extends all the way through to the other characters: Mr. Dalton is blindly philanthropic toward the very black man he exploits by overcharging his victims for the rat-infested tenements that they inhabit and that he owns; Jan Erlone and Mary Dalton are each blind in their own way as to what and who Bigger Thomas is or represents; certainly, the vigilante-like mob that roars for Bigger's life outside the jailhouse is blind with hatred—not so much of Bigger but of what he, in their hate-filled minds, represents for them; and Max, the Communist lawyer, is blind because all he can see in Bigger is the victim victimized by his society. Were the scales lifted from Max's eyes, he would be shocked—as he eventually is—to learn that Bigger's one exalted moment of freedom was that point in time when he had truly escaped the trammels of his society by destroying the person who represented the double standard and ambiguity of that society.

Even in the ghetto, Bigger cannot seem to escape the Daltons, who own the very tenement house Bigger lives in with his mother, brother, and sister. There (in the ghetto) he is trapped, finally, irrevocably:

He looked round the street and saw a sign on a building: THIS PROPERTY IS MANAGED BY THE SOUTH SIDE REAL ESTATE COMPANY. . . . He paid eight dollars a week for one rat-infested room. He had never seen Mr. Dalton until he had come to work for him; his mother always took the rent to the real estate office. Mr. Dalton was somewhere far away, high up, distant, like a god. He owned property all over the Black Belt. . . . Even though Mr. Dalton gave millions of dollars for Negro education, he would rent houses to Negroes only in this prescribed area, this corner of the city tumbling down from rot. (p. 148)

Finally, the labyrinth Bigger tries to escape from is more than the city; it is a condition—of his mind, of his inarticulateness, which, like the city itself, creates a labyrinth of its own.

In the manhunt for Bigger—another route Wright's naturalism takes—one senses that this is no hunt for a man but for an animal. Once the hunt gets under way, Bigger acts impulsively, from fear. Fear, which precedes escape, now builds to, and impels, that escape—takes it over, as it were. In almost every plan of escape discussed previously—and they have all virtually been prototypal escapes—there is at least some vague plan on the part of the escaper; even Lieutenant Henry in *A Farewell to Arms,* though initially impelled by fear of the Italian military police, knows, when he thinks things over in retrospect, that he will be on his way to Milan, away from the war—a plan that he vaguely senses will eventually lead him out of Italy itself. Bigger has no such plan or even a hope for one—for where would he go? Fear is the governing agency, to the extent that it eliminates rationality and puts in its place the kind of fantasizing that has led him into his impasse in the first place. Thus, his fear and anger, and the fantasy that grows out of them, are, before and after the climactic escape, the moving forces of Bigger's life.

As the police dragnet tightens around Bigger's hideout— "Surround the block," yells one of his pursuers—the pursuers themselves become animals—predators—stalking prey rather than game. As they move in for the kill, they themselves seem hostile to law, peace, and order. Their "shouts of wild joy" sound strangely incongruous for these appointed (or self-appointed?) defenders of the public weal. Like Bigger's, their feelings also seem to be a blend of fear, hatred, and sadism, so that they are white doubles, as it were, to Bigger. Where Bigger fears whiteness, these "guardians of the law" fear blackness. The difference between them and Bigger, however, is essentially one of status rather than personality or motivation. But for his color, Bigger might easily have found himself among the hunters rather than in the (black) skin of the hunted.

After he murders Bessie, Bigger's consciousness of whiteness becomes overwhelming. He observes that the streets are covered with a thick blanket of snow. But white does not only describe the non-color of snow; it is the color of the larger world beyond the ghetto, a world against which Bigger, like an unprepared fighting cock, has been pitted. He now sees whiteness all about him: in the blur of the blizzard, in Mary Dalton's mother, in the white cat in the Dalton household, omnipresent like Poe's black cat and possibly serving a similar sense of foreboding. And, finally, the whiteness is there in the faces of real enemies and would-be friends. What we have here is the reverse image of Melville's "power of blackness ten times black" made over into its white counterpart, for after Bessie's murder, whiteness for Bigger is something to run from, no matter in what shape or form it comes.

In the act of running away, Bigger learns that the white world, as symbolized by the snow-blanketed streets, is everywhere—that wherever he runs, he will be brought up short, confronted by the very world he is trying to flee. In sum, for Bigger, there is no way of escaping the white world short of death.

Where the other escapers in this study have used flight as a means of escaping untenable situations, flight for Bigger becomes more than a means; it is an end, whose purpose is to break through the mask of unreal reality—to break through one's existence as a "cipher," as Robert Bone calls Bigger, in order that he may find himself as a man and as an individual. Says Bone:

> [Bigger] has moved beyond the law, beyond convention, beyond good and evil, and he is now able to see beyond the surfaces of things. His sudden release [or escape] from the invisible forces that oppress him propels him toward a deeper vision of reality.[10]

Yet Bigger—like Huck Finn, Frederic Henry, John Andrews, Tom Joad, and Jake Blount—is also in flight from the law. (It is amazing how many escapers flee the law in their effort to escape the gravitational pull of the society that they have injured, but more important, that has injured them!) Yet although there is something pastoral in the escapes of those other escapers, Bigger never for one moment considers escape from the urban area into the "garden"—even before the necessity for such a decision arises. His escape remains concentrated within the labyrinth of the black ghetto. Even a Jake Blount can move from town to town—and his plight is *almost* as hopeless as Bigger's. Not so Bigger. Like the rat in the early part of the book, he is trapped in a closed society.

Further, where other escape novels climax with the escape itself, in *Native Son* escape, as such, is not climactic; it is central both in the formal structure of the novel (Part II, "Escape") and in Bigger's heart. It is not simply a means but an end. Yet, end as it well may be, Bigger eventually comes to find himself in a place from which any escape is impossible. His flight (or attempted flight) forms the bridge from one prison (ghetto) to another (the literal prison and, eventually, the death house in that prison).

Like Huck, who puts his interrogators off the trail by various devices of dissimulation, so Bigger, in the first step of his flight after Mary Dalton's murder, decides to use the Communist pamphlets that Jan Erlone had given him to put his pursuers off his scent and point the finger of suspicion at Erlone and his Party friends. His desperation, then, not only makes for flight but for a certain crude, though desperate, ingenuity.

Again like Huck, Bigger is an escaper from a hypocritical society: the Dalton's and their philanthropy remind one keenly of Aunt Sally and her family, who can also treat black men, "philanthropically" (in their own fashion) yet be capable of subjecting them to the degradation of slavery. To this extent, Bigger's twentieth-century society has not moved any appreciable distance from Huck's.

Like Tom Joad, but not for the same reasons, Bigger kills. Unlike Tom, however, who kills the first time in self-defense and second in a spirit of avenging retribution, Bigger kills out of a mixture of fear and anger. Yet in both Tom's and Bigger's instances, the killings precipitate escapes—from the law at first remove and from society generally. Like Cain, whose name these escapers bear, they are doomed to wander the earth, ever seeking a haven they are unable to find, ever hoping for the rest that never comes, ever dreaming the dream that will never materialize. Thus, both Tom Joad and Bigger Thomas are the products of their respective societies, as to a lesser degree the other escapers are.[11] For abuse from without leads to alienation from within. And the one word to describe the condition of the escape-murderer is alienation, as battered and worn a verbal catchall as that word has become

Like Jake Blount's escape in *The Heart is a Lonely Hunter,* Bigger's too is without hope—except that in Bigger's case, he knows there is no hope. Perhaps in this sense, Bigger's is the truer victory, for he fights on even after he knows the cards have been stacked against him—surely a heroic act under any circumstances. Unlike Blount in the other novel (whose action ironically takes place in the South, from which Bigger's family —such as it is—had come), Bigger *chooses* not to hope. In this respect, Bigger was already an "existentialist" before either the word (in its contemporary sense) or the philosophy it referred to had become fashionable. The loss of hope in Bigger becomes transformed into a vow: "A small hard core in him resolved never again to trust anybody or anything. . . . Whatever he thought or did from now on would have to come from him and him alone, or not at all" (p. 289).

The book ends as it began. In the beginning, Bigger is caged *within* the labyrinth of his urban society; by the time we get to the end of the book, he is still caged, but now *by* his society. And although *Native Son* has been seen as crude in its technique—a black proletarian novel wherein the departure or escape lies in the hero's *non*-salvation—this work is probably the most powerful statement of rebellion and escape that has been made in the American novel in the first half of the twentieth century.

1. Richard Wright, *Native Son* (New York, 1940), p. 17. Used with the permission of Harper & Row, Publishers. All further quotations are taken from this edition.

2. Not that rebellion as such (even in Bigger's sense) is absolutely without some satisfaction, if we take into account Frantz Fanon's concept of violent rebellion as therapeutic act, as set forth in his *Wretched of the Earth*. By fruitless, we mean of course the rebellion that has as its objective a realizable goal within the larger social cosmos—even at the risk that that realization may well be vitiated by the very rebellion (or reaction to it) that set out to reach that (realizable) goal.

3. Harry Slochower, *No Voice Is Wholly Lost* (London, 1946), p. 88.

4. Edwin Berry Burgum, *The Novel and the World's Dilemma* (New York, 1947), p. 234.

5. Robert Bone, *Richard Wright* (Minneapolis, Minn., 1964), p. 21.

6. Albert Camus, *The Rebel* (New York, 1956), p. 20. Used with the permission of Alfred A. Knopf, Inc.

7. Ibid., p. 15.

8. Ibid., p. 17.

9. Ibid., p. 14.

10. Bone, p. 21.

11. It has been noted that Bigger's name has a kind of counter-symbolism as Tom Joad's does not. That is, Bigger is no *Uncle* Tom, but a bigger—the small "b" is no typographical error!—Thomas. That is, he is a larger-than-life figure. However, even Tom Joad's name bears a certain symbolism in that it is an assonantal echo of John Doe—a kind of Everyman-in-the-street whose name (among poor Oklahoma sharecroppers) will become legion.

chapter ten

Flight:
Some Conclusions

"If things become unbearable . . .
go somewhere else."
—Edward T. Bowden,
The Dungeon of the Heart

As I hope I have shown, the current of escape that runs through the modern American novel runs broad and deep. Generally, the escapes are from societies and their specific evils —war, injustice, the encroachments on the individual sensibility. Involved also is the flight from an earlier, innocent self, a discovery of a new reality (or simply *reality,* as opposed to pristine innocence). Concomitantly, it also involves a growing (and conscious) rejection of former values, and finally a denial of one's former life. As corollary, these flights may also involve a flight *toward* maturity, *toward* a new life, *toward* a search for a new identity (or perhaps for an earlier identity).

In view of these criteria, how effective, then, have the escapes been? Can we draw some tentative conclusions from our findings? Edward T. Bowden makes one observation about the impulse to escape that makes its own valid point. Bowden here uses George Willard as his example, but the example may be taken as a paradigm for all escapers in the modern American novel:

> If things become unbearable . . . go somewhere else. . . . George [Willard] . . . is escaping from Winesburg, but one suspects that the escape is for him . . . only a temporary one. Death would seem the only really complete escape from life, but death is too final an answer.[1]

Of course "death is too final an answer"! It eliminates any possibililty of rebirth—on this plane. From this kind of "out" nothing can obviously be gained—either for the escaper or for the literature that celebrates him. The concomitant of escape implies that the escaper has learned something from the experience—if only negatively.

All of the escapers discussed in the preceding pages seem to display a common element: they are either individuals who have had—so they thought—strong beliefs that they are no longer able to believe in, or they are impulsively reacting to what *was,* in the hope of finding something better. These run the gamut from Huck Finn, with his initial trust in the shibboleths and customs of a hypocritical society, to Preacher Casy and his exchange of an earlier, simpler belief for a more socially conscious vision. Only Bigger Thomas's escape is, in its long range sense, an act of desperation rather than hope.

About half of the escapers we have discussed move west: Huck Finn (to the Territory), Theron Ware (to Seattle), George Willard (to "the city"—presumably Chicago), and the Joads (to California). Their escapes, unlike those of Frederick Henry, John Andrews, Jake Blount, and Bigger Thomas, have an element of hope in them, no matter how tenuous that hope may be. Out West, they seem to feel, they will find what they thought to be lacking where they came from.

But hopeful or not, the escapes are more than just escapes; where successful, or even, ambiguously, semisuccessful, they suggest—symbolically for the most part—a form of rebirth. Three of these are achieved by the conventionally ritualistic (i.e., symbolic) immersion in water: Huck into the Mississippi; Lieutenant Henry into the Tagliamento; and John Andrews into the Seine. Jake Blount's escape may be likened to the motions of a karmic wheel (like the flying jinny he operates) whose turnings lead from one life into another, though not necessarily a better, one. Bigger Thomas's escape is perhaps the most hopeless of the lot, restricted, as it is, to the prison (the ghetto labyrinth) of his larger society. Bigger's escape, we know, is doomed from the start. We can afford greater optimism toward the efforts of Bigger's companions in the fraternity of flight in the American novel.

Tom Joad is reborn, but Steinbeck deliberately seems to have kept his destination—though not his destiny—ambiguous (since Tom intends to blend in with the "social soul"). Of all the escapers, Tom has tied his goal to the larger cause of that "soul," to the destiny of "the people," with whom he finally identifies, and with whom he aims to merge. His escape is thus more explicitly spiritual than geographical, though of course virtually all of the escapers discussed in this study need to embark on a geographical journey in order to reach some sort of spiritual destination.

Huck lights out into the Territory. But even if his escape is not a permanent one, it does represent—perhaps even coincides with—the escapes of those who moved West when that movement was beginning to get under way. Jake Blount's escape, on the other hand, is a weakening of the force that inspired the Westward Movement in the first place. His escape is a limited one—a wandering from one southern town to another. Although Huck will return to the society he has left behind, his escape, limited as it is, does at least suggest new beginnings. When he returns to that society he will not be the boy who fled it; psychologically he will have entered manhood. Blount's escape, on the other hand, suggests no substantive growth. Indeed, his escapes have led from one dead-end town to another: they represent a spiritual cul-de-sac; he seems to have learned nothing from his traumatic experiences.

Huck's escape is perhaps the most comprehensive; for it virtually rejects every aspect of a society that thrives on violence, hypocrisy (manifest in its inflated rhetoric), and the degradation of black people. Indeed, the more orotund the rhetoric, the less one can trust what it attempts to defend— the slave society. And Huck comes by this knowledge painfully —as all who mistake rhetoric for reality must.

According to Lauriat Lane, the escapes of Huck and Jim are futile since their significance lies not so much in their achievement—or more to the point, lack of it—but in what each of the escapers has learned from the experience. Yet if the escapers have indeed gained something from the experience, then the gains have surely outweighed the futility of their escapes or their attempts. In truth, Huck's escape is open-ended. It is left (deliberately?) ambiguous and unresolved. As R. P. Adams suggests, the true conclusion of the story—and Huck's escape along with it—is its very inconclusiveness:

> The impression Clemens has to leave, and does leave, in the reader's mind and feelings is that Huck will continue to develop. He will escape again, as many times as he needs to, from society and any of its restrictions which would hamper and prevent his growth. He will die and be reborn whenever his character needs to break the mold that society would place upon it. Accordingly, the structure of the story is left open: *the conclusion is deliberately inconclusive.*[2]

According to Albert E. Stone, "Huck's quest for freedom cannot succeed"[3] whether because of the river whose current carries him farther south into slave territory or because of the accidents of fogs and floods. But such phrases as "the quest for freedom" and "escape" need some qualification.

It has been suggested that Huck doesn't really make good his escape to the Territory (in the sense of a satisfactory resolution) but intends—consciously or not—to return to St. Petersburg, as indeed he does in *Tom Sawyer Abroad* (1894), where both he and Tom will be whisked across the Atlantic by a mad balloonist, and thence across the Sahara. Wished-for or not, this episode is another version of escape, though it hardly has the symbolic resonance of a *Huckleberry Finn.*

Yet in spite of Huck's transatlantic adventure, the suggestion of escape is still relatively valid; for at the encouragement of Tom, he has left St. Petersburg behind, and in doing so he foreshadows the later transatlantic expatriate-escaper of the twenties.

Like Lauriat Lane and Albert Stone, Leslie Fiedler also
suggests that Huck's escape is in vain: Huck "does not know
to *what* he is escaping, except into nothing. . . . Huck is heading for no utopia, since he has heard of none; and so he ends up
making the flight itself his goal. . . . [His escape] of course
. . . is a vain evasion except as it leads him to understand that
no society can fulfill his destiny." [4] In this sense all of our
escapes end there. Freud, to whom Fiedler is partly indebted,
amply supports the notion of a return to beginnings—in short,
regression. Yet the value of escape lies not so much in its ends
as in its means (or in the experience). There are those, of
course, who do not learn from experience. Jake Blount is one,
and, perhaps at a greater remove, Theron Ware. Curiously,
Bigger Thomas, whose escape is the most hopeless, seems to
have gained by his escape (more an act of personal liberation
than of classic escape) a new realization of the inner drives and
mechanisms of his old and new self. But perplexity is part of
the human predicament: for an escape may as often prove to be
an entrance into a new trap, or an old prison, as a way out of
it—as indeed it becomes for Bigger Thomas.

According to Walter F. Taylor,[5] Theron Ware's escape is
another of those unsuccessful bids for freedom. But we must
remember that Theron's escape is not so much from a society—
he will probably end up in the same sort of sorry milieu he has
left—as from one way of life (or life-style) into another. Thus,
Theron's escape is only partly successful. Among those elements
he wished to escape (apart from his ministry) were Alice, his
wife, and the marriage that bound him to her. Ironically, she
accompanies Theron out West, ever a reminder of his more innocent self and the days of his more audacious desires—but also
a reminder that he is still bound to her!

George Willard makes his escape a "revolt from the village."
But again, the conclusion—his departure from Winesburg—is

more suggestive than definitive. What is important is not that the escapers have specific plans—perhaps the plan, if any, suggests what they are escaping *from*—but that they make the escape at all. In this instance, then, the desire rather than the fulfillment is what is important.

John Andrews escapes from the regimentation of modern life as represented by the army. But his escape is ultimately unsuccessful. Again, it is the intention rather than its consummation that is important. Actually, Andrews's predicament is more personal than universal. Certainly, his plight is not nearly as critical as that of Lieutenant Henry or Tom Joad, and certainly nothing to compare to Bigger Thomas's. Although, like Henry, Tom and Bigger, he may be said to be a "prisoner" of the system, his tendency to indulge in hysterics tends to overplay (and therefore to undercut) those horrors of regimentation that lie, not so much in their tedium—which can be endured—as in the manner in which the tedium itself is filtered through Andrews's mind.

Lieutenant Henry's escape from the war and its senselessness is partly successful, and carries a greater resonance than does that of Andrews. Henry's hope that Catherine would live "is as illusory as his belief that he could escape the war by signing a separate peace." [6] Ray B. West's conclusion here is that one cannot "escape," in the existential sense, the consequence of an action: "What [*A Farewell to Arms*] says, finally, is that you cannot escape the obligations of [an] action. . . . You can only learn to live with life, to tolerate it as 'the initiated' learn to tolerate it." [7]

Tom Joad not only escapes from the law (specifically) but also from what James Baldwin might call a "previous condition." His escape is not so much from the society itself as it is a merging with that society (the social soul). Actually, it is an escape back into society, not so much to accept as to fight it

—or at least to fight its seamier aspects. His escape, unlike those of the other escapers, is not an outright rejection of society—Joad is no revolutionary—but a desire to get society to make some urgently needed changes. In *The Grapes of Wrath* there is at least some slight hope that things will get better, as compared with the near nihilistic despair at the end of *A Farewell to Arms*. Both novels conclude in rain, symbol of death in each. In *A Farewell to Arms* death ends the last scene—as it usually does!—both for Catherine and her still-born baby. But in *The Grapes of Wrath* there is the suggestion that Rose of Sharon will survive both the depression of the times as well as of the heart. Peter Lisca maintains, "Out of her need [Rose of Sharon] gives life [the milk-full breast she offers the starving man]. . . . Out of the profoundest depth of despair comes the greatest assertion of faith." [8]

Jake Blount's escape in *The Heart is a Lonely Hunter* tells us, as we have noted, of Jake's bankruptcy of hope. Quite simply, Jake no longer has any territorial frontiers to escape across. He has been born too late for a frontier and perhaps too early for his version of the American (proletarian) dream. Jake's escape is therefore the least effective (in terms of the success of his revolutionary goals) of any of the escapes we have discussed. Whereas most of the escapers have changed, or have been transformed by their experiences—Huck, reborn through the discovery of his heart; Andrews and Henry, through their separate peace; Willard, through youth to early manhood; Tom Joad, through his vision of social unity; Theron Ware, through a new knowledge (painfully acquired) of his limitations—Jake Blount remains essentially what he was before he fled town. His escape is illusory. Where the other escapers have some idea of where they are bound—even if they don't always succeed in getting there—Blount has no idea of where he is going. Thus, his escape is symbolically, if not liter-

ally and geographically, circular; he will end up in the same
kind of town he has left—and probably, with his frayed ideal-
ism, repeat all of the futile motions.

Still, if there is any escape that is more hopeless than
Blount's, it is Bigger Thomas's. Of all the escapers, notwithstanding Sinclair Lewis's prescription (that the escaper not
only needs a "place from which to flee but a place to which to
flee"), Bigger has no place to escape *to*. His escape is not
merely circular, as in Blount's case, but, as was suggested in
the preceding chapter, labyrinthine, moving ever inward on
itself, so that Bigger meets himself on the way out and falls
into the hands of the law, that legal trap provided by the society
that has driven him into the labyrinth in the first place. Where
Blount's escape, futile as it is, held out some small hope (or so
Blount believes), Bigger's is completely without that small
saving quality. Bigger himself, even in the process of running
away, knows well enough that his flight is doomed even before
it begins.

Finally, escape seems to express the discrepancy between
what life is and what it could be—in the minds of the escapers
at least. It is also a manifestation of the dislocation of life in its
transition from the latter decades of the nineteenth century
to the early decades of the twentieth—as noted so mordantly by
Henry Adams in his *Education.*

In our time—roughly the fifties to the seventies—this
universal experience, particularly as it has been dealt with by
the Jewish-American writer, attests to the possibility of other
forms of escape. Leslie Fiedler says:

All flights, the Jewish experience teaches, are from one exile to
another; and this Americans have always known, though they
have sometimes attempted to deny it. Fleeing exclusion in the
Old World, the immigrant discovers loneliness in the New
World; fleeing the communal loneliness of seaboard settlements,

he discovers the ultimate isolation of the frontier. It is the dream of exile as freedom which has made America; but it is [also] the experience of exile as terror that has forged the self-consciousness of Americans.[9]

Yet for whatever reason—out of hope or hopelessness—escape seems to be as much an "inalienable right" as those other guaranteed rights Americans have usually taken for granted. Still, we must not forget that the "guarantees" are provisional. The following little anecdote of Robert Frost is as illustrative of this (essentially youthful) impulse as any we have shown here, and it is a fitting note on which to end:

A young fellow came to me to complain of the department of philosophy in his university. There wasn't a philosopher in it. "I can't stand it." He was really complaining of his situation. He wasn't where he could feel real. But I didn't tell him so [;] I didn't go into that. I agreed with him that there wasn't a philosopher in his university—there was hardly ever more than one at a time in the world—and I advised him to quit. Light out for somewhere. He hated to be a quitter. I told him the Bible says, "Quit ye, like men." "Does it," he said. "Where would I go?" Why anywhere almost. Kamchatka, Madagascar, Brazil. I found him doing well in the educational department of Rio when I was sent on an errand down there by our government several years later.[10]

1. Edward T. Bowden, *The Dungeon of the Heart: Human Isolation and the American Novel* (New York, 1961), pp. 121–22.

2. R. P. Adams, "Why *Huckleberry Finn* Is a Great American Novel," in *Mark Twain's Huckleberry Finn,* ed. Barry Marks (Boston, 1959), pp. 99–100; italics added.

3. Albert E. Stone, *The Innocent Eye: Childhood in Mark Twain's Imagination* (New Haven, Conn., 1961), p. 143.

4. Leslie A. Fiedler, *Love and Death in the American Novel* (New York, 1960), p. 582.

5. "Fiction and Social Debate," in *Literary History of the United States,* ed. Robert E. Spiller et al., rev. ed. (New York, 1963).

6. Ray B. West, Jr., "A Farewell to Arms," in *Ernest Hemingway: Critiques of Four Major Novels,* ed. Carlos Baker (New York, 1962), p. 34. Used by permission of Charles Scribner's Sons.

7. Ibid., p. 36.

8. Peter Lisca, *The Wide World of John Steinbeck* (New Brunswick, N.J., 1958), p. 177. Critics have generally deplored this unrealistic (i.e., implausible) denouement, especially its sentimentality. But we can ignore the sentimentality—admittedly there—in favor of the symbolic redemption of hope in a time of hopelessness. As such, the scene has its valid place in a novel that, though told in the naturalist tradition, is nevertheless saturated with mythopoeia.

9. Leslie A. Fiedler, *Waiting for the End* (New York, 1964), pp. 83–84.

10. Robert Frost, "On Emerson," *Daedalus* (Fall, 1959); reprinted in *Emerson,* ed. Milton Konvitz and Stephen Whicher (Englewood Cliffs, N.J., 1962), p. 12.

Below is a checklist of novels that include or touch on an escape of one sort or another. A number of these escapes are significantly decisive for the escapers, leaving their marks, or even scars, on them; some are only ancillary to the wider, and presumably more important, activities of a character. One of these escapes is fully intended, planned, but abortive, as is that of Hester Prynne and Arthur Dimmesdale in *The Scarlet Letter*. Some are only of brief duration, an interlude in the lives of those who make the attempt, but who later return home—somewhat chastened, perhaps—to take up their lives where they had left them. But all have one thing in common: a desire —yearned for or consummated—to cut present moorings in order to learn what lies beyond the horizon of the future. In doing so, the escapers perhaps learn something, as much about themselves as they do about life and the world beyond the peripheries of their immediate environment.

I. Pre-*Huckleberry Finn*

Note: Names in parentheses are those of the escaper or escapers; these may not always be major characters, but the larger number are.

Charles Brockden Brown. *Edgar Huntly; or, Memoirs of a Sleepwalker,* 1799 (Clithero Edny).

James Fenimore Cooper. *The Pioneers,* 1823 (Natty Bumppo).

———. *The Prairie,* 1827 (Ishmael Bush and his family).

———. *The Spy,* 1821 (Captain Henry Wharton).

Nathaniel Hawthorne. *The House of the Seven Gables,* 1851 (Clifford and Hepzibah Pyncheon).

———. *The Scarlet Letter,* 1850 (Hester Prynne and Arthur Dimmesdale).

William Dean Howells. *A Modern Instance,* 1882 (Bartley Hubbard).

Helen Hunt Jackson. *Ramona,* 1884 (Ramona, Alessandro).

Henry James. *The American,* 1877 (Claire de Cintre).

Herman Melville. *Moby Dick,* 1851 (Ishmael).

———. *Typee,* 1846 (Tom, an American sailor; Toby, the same).

Harriet Beecher Stowe. *Dred: A Tale of the Great Dismal Swamp,* 1856 (Harry Gordon).

———. *Uncle Tom's Cabin,* 1852 (Eliza and George Harris).

John Townsend Trowbridge. *Cudjo's Cave,* 1863 (Penn Hapgood).

———. *Neighbor Jackwood,* 1856 (Camille "Milly" Delisard).

II. 1885 and After

Sherwood Anderson. *Dark Laughter,* 1925 (John Stockton).

Gertrude Atherton. *Julia France and Her Times,* 1912 (Julia Edis France).

Louis Bromfield. *Escape,* a tetralogy: *The Green Bay Tree,* 1924; *Possession,* 1925; *Early Autumn,* 1926; *A Good Woman,* 1927 (various characters).

Willa Cather. *Sapphira and the Slave Girl,* 1940 (Nancy Till).

Walter Van Tilburg Clark. *The Ox-Bow Incident,* 1940 (Art Croft and Gil Carter).

Samuel Langhorne Clemens (Mark Twain). *Pudd'nhead Wilson,* 1894 (Roxy and Chambers).

Floyd Dell. *Moon Calf,* 1920 (Felix Fay).

John Dos Passos. *Manhattan Transfer,* 1925 (Jimmy Herf).

———. *U.S.A.,* a trilogy: *The Forty-Second Parallel,* 1930; *1919,* 1932; *The Big Money,* 1936 (various characters).

Theodore Dreiser. *Sister Carrie,* 1900 (Carrie Meebers; Hurstwood).

William Faulkner. *Absalom, Absalom!,* 1936 (Henry Sutpen).

———. *Light in August,* 1932 (Joe Christmas; Joe Brown, alias Lucas Burch).

———. *The Sound and the Fury,* 1929 (Quentin, daughter of Candace Compson).

F. Scott Fitzgerald. *Tender is the Night,* 1934 (Dick Diver).

Zona Gale. *Miss Lulu Bett,* 1920 (Lulu Bett).

Hamlin Garland. *Rose of Dutcher's Coolly,* 1895 (Rose Dutcher).

Ellen Glasgow. *Barren Ground,* 1925 (Dorinda Oakley).

———. *Virginia,* 1913 (Oliver Treadwell).

———. *The Romantic Comedians,* 1926 (Annabel Upchurch).

A. B. Guthrie, Jr. *The Big Sky,* 1947 (Boone Caudill).

Joseph Heller. *Catch-22,* 1961 (Orr).

Ernest Hemingway. *The Sun Also Rises,* 1926 (the major characters).

William Dean Howells. *The Rise of Silas Lapham,* 1885 (Silas and Persis Lapham; Tom Corey and Penelope Lapham).

Jack Kerouac. *On The Road,* 1957 (Dean Moriarty).

Ken Kesey. *One Flew Over the Cuckoo's Nest,* 1962 (Broom "Chief" Bromden).

Sinclair Lewis. *Main Street,* 1920 (Carol Kennicott).

Bernard Malamud. *A New Life,* 1961 (Levin).

Frank Norris. *McTeague,* 1899 (McTeague).

———. *The Octopus,* 1901 (Presley).

David Graham Phillips. *Susan Lenox: Her Fall and Rise,* 1917 (Susan Lenox).

Conrad Richter. *The Sea of Grass,* 1936 (Lutie Cameron Brewton).

———. *The Town,* 1950 (Chancey and Guerdon Wheeler).

Elizabeth M. Roberts. *The Time of Man,* 1926 (Ellen Chesser Kent; Jasper Kent).

J. D. Salinger. *Catcher in the Rye,* 1951 (Holden Caulfield).

George Santayana. *The Last Puritan,* 1936 (Oliver Alden).

Upton Sinclair. *The Jungle,* 1906 (Jurgis Rudkus).

Lillian Smith. *Strange Fruit,* 1944 (Ed Anderson).

Robert Penn Warren. *All the King's Men,* 1946 (Jack Burden).

Nathanael West. *Miss Lonelyhearts,* 1933 (Willie Shrike, as he describes various modes of escape).

Thomas Wolfe. *Look Homeward, Angel: A Story of the Buried Life,* 1929 (Eugene Gant).